Character is Destiny

Pat Hews

Pen Press Publishers Ltd

First published in Great Britain by
Pen Press Publishers Ltd
39-41, North Road
Islington
London N7 9DP

ISBN 1-905203-53-5

Printed and bound in the UK

A catalogue record of this book is available from
the British Library

Cover Illustration by Jacqueline Abromeit

To my husband John with my love

Contents

Acknowledgement

The Salesians Family, founded by Don Bosco

PROLOGUE

The man was a stranger to me and, consequently, of very little interest. With the wisdom of a well-adjusted seven-year-old I gave him no more than a quick glance and brief smile before getting on with my young life.

Certainly I was aware that this was my father, the man whom I had heard much of and seen little. Occasionally he had visited for a day or two and, to please my mother, I had written a few short letters to be sent to him somewhere overseas. More recently we had visited him at the local hospital where hushed voices had echoed around the long shining corridors and I had quickly escaped to the gardens to play with the other children.

Apparently 'he' was going to live with us now and as my mother seemed very happy about the arrangements I was not particularly bothered one way or the other. At least I had not been bothered until I realised that this stranger was actually interfering in our lives. He planned to move us, lock, stock, barrel and dog from our village home to the bombsites of London.

Throughout the British Isles, in fact throughout Europe, many young families were attempting to come to terms with

1

a stranger suddenly appearing on the scene and invading their established milieu. Children who, until the summer of 1945, had been growing up within a single parent family unit, a world apart from the modern acceptance of a one parent family. Counselling was not in fashion and so parents and children muddled through fairly successfully given the time, the place and the conditions.

Of course there were many whose loved-ones would never return from war. Others, unable to remember the virile young men who had so bravely marched away to set the world free, would spend much of their young lives tending the broken mind or body of a stranger called father.

The journey to London was long if uneventful. Father had left some weeks earlier and was already living and working in the capital. Somehow, and for some obscure reason, my brother had persuaded everyone that he should stay behind, spending a few months with friends in the area while continuing his education at the Wellingborough Grammar School.

Meanwhile my mother lifted me and the dog unceremoniously on to the furniture van where we both huddled together in the only available space, over the engine casing.

London was everything I had expected, large, concrete, dirty and in various stages of devastation. It was a very long time before I forgave my father for taking me away from village life; the fields where I had chased rabbits with Prince, our mongrel dog, the haystacks where we had often hidden from the local farmer and the woodland where we had played so happily our games of make-believe.

In the years that followed I came to know the man who was my father! An amazing and fascinating man! Adventure had been his bedfellow virtually from the day he was born. Many of his daring escapades were kept as close secrets, jealously guarded from his offspring in fear that they may, one day, attempt to emulate his exploits. This was indubitably an impossibility since the ever-changing scenes and circumstances of my father's life were unique and the lessons to be learned infinite.

In recent years I have found photographs and documents that tell the true story of Dick Cooper. A story that is proof in itself that character is destiny and that many of today's social theories and practices are just plain and simple bunkum.

1 Abducted

A piercing scream soared from an open window and seemed to echo around the slender spires of the minarets, reaching skyward from the dusty streets of Baghdad.

Passers-by hesitated, looking with interest towards the imposing residence in the European quarter of the town from where the sounds had come. Nearby the Tigris flowed peacefully on its way as it had done since time immemorial, oblivious of the sudden heart-rending cry.

For a moment there was silence. Then a pitiful moan was quickly followed by the sound of a woman sobbing uncontrollably. The bustle of the street below paused momentarily as traders and pilgrims alike were struck by the tragic sounds.

In the room above, a tearful Arab servant crossed to the open window and quietly closed the shutters. Behind her, a well dressed woman lay sobbing into a counterpane that draped a luxurious double bed. Now, in half darkness, the servant dared to beg for forgiveness while tears streamed down her own face and her hunched shoulders jerked up and down in despair.

Having heard the commotion from his study, Arthur Cooper raced to the room. Looking across at his wife Arthur caught his breath, appreciating once again the beauty of her outline as she lay face down before him. Elenora Cooper was a lovely young woman. Her lineage could be traced back to the thirteenth century, the dark hair betraying the Italian connection and the sparkle in her eyes revealing the Irish wit and charm. Arthur had first met her in Beirut where his family lived. More recently the young couple had moved to Baghdad due to Arthur's appointment as an inspector with the Tombac Tobacco Company.

The Cooper family had lived in the Middle East since 1860 when Arthur's father had joined the Eastern Telegraph Company as an engineer. Europeans were assured of a welcome, a very good income and consequently an excellent standard of living which gave them every incentive to stay.

Elenora heard his footsteps as he crossed the room. She leapt from the bed and fell into his outstretched arms. Drawing in short sharp breaths, while her unchecked tears soaked his sombre tie, she tried to tell him the reason for her anguish.

"He's gone," she wailed.

"Who has gone?" Arthur looked around the room his eyes appealing to the tearful maid for help.

"Bebo," she cried. "My baby! They stole him!"

Elenora had given birth to their third child on the 28th February 1899. Like his brother and sister, the boy had automatically taken the British nationality of his father and his birth had been registered under his full name, Adolphe Richard, at the Consulate-General in Baghdad.

Adolphe was now six months old and an obvious target for the unscrupulous travellers that frequented the bazaars of Baghdad. Arthur needed no further bidding. He grabbed the servant by her shoulder and shouted, "Where is he? What have you done you stupid girl?" Seeing the subject of his

5

wrath collapse at his feet, Arthur stepped over her, shouting at the top of his voice for Farez, senior servant to the household and husband of the offending woman.

With the help of Farez the chain of events began unfold. Questioning the girl, who had only recently been appointed nanny to the three children, the two men found they had little information to go on. The woman admitted to leaving the child sleeping in his pram outside a shop close to the local Bazaar. Minutes later she had emerged to find the pram empty with the dainty canopy laying crumpled on the ground. For a while she had run up and down the twisting complex of streets and alleyways, wasting valuable time while the abductor had presumably moved purposefully out of the town.

In fact, an unsavoury group of travellers had been scouring the suburbs of Baghdad, stealing as they went. One member of their group had seized the opportunity to grab the child by his silk nightdress and thrust him into the folds of his own filthy robe. It was easy to vanish with the help of his colleagues. They were adept at splitting up to block the way of any would be followers.

The kidnapper was a man called Hassan. He and his friends were on their travels from the interior of Saudi Arabia into Mesopotamia. Knowing that the Turkish police would soon be alerted to the kidnap the man made his way to Karbala on the edge of the Syrian Desert with the intention of hiding out for a while.

Hassan was determined to hold the child for ransom, which would provide him with a better return than selling him. Meanwhile baby Adolphe proved to be a handful for the inexperienced abductor. The more the child was ignored the more he screamed for attention. The man was on the verge of abandoning the whole idea when he met up with a young

Moroccan girl who fussed and cooed over the baby until the little one smiled and cooed back at her. Hassan was quick to appreciate the silence and promised the girl good money if she cared for the child. The three of them then waited at Karbala for other members of Hassan's group to join them. More than a month passed and eventually they gave up waiting and travelled south to winter in the district of El Batn.

Before very long the young Moroccan girl had fallen completely under the spell of the pale skinned child who had dark brown eyes like her own. The boy was fed on milk from goats and camels and was treated as a native. Before long his skin became deeply bronzed and after seven months it was impossible to recognise him as a European. The Moroccan girl became very attached to the baby, thinking of him as her own child. She was fiercely possessive if anyone tried to interfere, particularly Hassan.

This was not part of the plan and Hassan knew he had to break up the happy little family. Deciding that sufficient time had passed since he had grabbed the boy, he made up his mind to return to Baghdad and demand a ransom. Once again he stole the child, this time in the middle of the night, silently creeping past the slumbering girl.

Adolphe, dressed in coarse Arab cloth, was uttering his first words in Arabic so it was unlikely anyone would suspect he was a missing European child. The two odd companions journeyed together for three months eventually reaching Mal-i-Mushrak, thirty-seven miles south of Baghdad.

Hassan had given a lot of thought to his plans, realising he needed some sort of partner to negotiate with the child's parents. There was a frustrating delay while he looked around, his attempts to care for the child being the most challenging of the tasks before him. Eventually he struck lucky in locating an old acquaintance, a shifty Armenian who was more than willing to assist him for a percentage of the ransom money.

It was with very little effort that they discovered the child was British. Both men were stunned. Great Britain was a huge and respected power in the world and the possible consequences of their actions did not bear thinking about. They argued and finally took refuge in drink, ending up in a stupor on the floor of the Armenian's home.

Meanwhile, instinct had told the Moroccan girl that something was wrong. The morning after Hassan had taken the child she had woken early with an empty feeling that seemed to tie an invisible knot in her stomach. Barefooted and wearing nothing but a cotton shift she had reached the child's makeshift cot only to find it empty. Little more than a child herself, the tears had trickled from her large dark eyes and there had been a haunting loveliness in her grief-stricken face.

Suddenly she had brushed aside the tears, pulled a coarse woven dress over her head and started to pick up a few essentials for her journey. Filling a rough sack with scraps of food, she had topped up a water bottle and tied the whole lot into a small blanket. Having tied a piece of material torn from the blanket's edge around her forehead, the girl had raced, anxious to cover a reasonable distance before the sun was high. She knew Hassan's destination, she had been waiting for him to make his move but somehow the crafty parasite had still managed to elude her.

Living and travelling by her wits, the young girl made reasonable progress in her search for the baby. Occasionally a caravan would catch up with her as she walked in the early morning and she would beg a ride on a camel. Once in a while she was able to gather news of Hassan's progress, confirming her self-adopted son survived and that somehow she was narrowing the distance between them. Eventually she reached Mal-i-Mushrak and was quick to establish that Hassan and the boy were still there.

Following the direction pointed out to her by a group of cackling women, the girl entered the house of the Armenian uninvited. She found Hassan and the little boy asleep on a pile of dirty rugs while the owner of the house was nowhere in sight.

Throwing caution to the wind, the young Moroccan raised her eyes to the heavens and chanted a series of joyful if unintelligible screeches, wakening the sleeping pair. The child smiled in delight reaching out his arms for the warmth and love awaiting him but before the girl could lift him to her, Hassan leapt at her in drunken fury. The frustration of the past months poured out of the man as he attacked the intruder with unwarranted ferocity. Knocked unconscious, the girl fell to the floor like a log. The child screamed in terror causing Hassan to panic and run from the house, quickly disappearing from sight.

Awakening to the screams, the young Moroccan dragged herself to her feet and staggered over to the child while blood dripped unnoticed from a vicious wound to her head. Their reunion could quite happily have gone on forever; such was the bond that had grown between these two young people from such different worlds. The interruption, when it came, was both sudden and frightening. The room was cast into darkness as the Armenian returned. As he stood in the doorway of his home, he blocked the light and their only route to freedom.

It was obvious to the newcomer that although the girl before him might be wounded and exhausted she would be ready to die before parting with her young charge. Luckily the man had been having some serious second thoughts about the scam and was more than happy to see the back of Hassan and the problems he had brought with him. Things were getting far too difficult and he had wanted to get out of the situation before serious trouble descended upon him and his household. With considerable relief he told the Moroccan everything they had discovered about the baby.

Her decision to return Adolphe to his family was agonising. The girl would be giving up everything she held precious. However it was because she loved the child so dearly that she was prepared to say goodbye to him, most likely forever. The rest of the journey to Baghdad was accomplished quickly in the company of a Bedouin and his sturdy donkeys.

Wearily the girl made her way to the office of the British Consulate General where she recounted this story. The original account of her deposition was sent to the British Embassy in Constantinople (now Istanbul) where, hopefully, it remains in safekeeping. A copy was handed to Arthur Cooper when he collected the child, who bore not the slightest resemblance to the baby who had been kidnapped. Luckily positive identification was made possible by two small birthmarks, in particular an unusual mark on the child's foot.

Alone and desolate the young girl stayed in Baghdad hoping to catch another glimpse of her baby. A few days had seemed like an eternity when suddenly the boy's father sought her out and offered her the job of nursemaid to all three of his children. It had been obvious to Arthur that it had taken considerable courage and an amazing strength of character for this woman to return the child to his home.

In the months that had passed since Bebo had been abducted, Elenora had undergone various stages of depression until she had come to neglect her husband and the two older children. This was a very headstrong woman whose ancestors included the Malatestas a half brigand, half condottiere family who had held Rimini in a tyrannical grip between the thirteenth and sixteenth centuries. The name of Count Malaspina could also be found within the branches of her family tree. She became self-centred, bitter, complaining and greedy. Finally she ran away with her husband's employer, Stanislaus Wroblenski, director of the Tombac Company and godfather to her youngest child. Arthur was devastated by her desertion. He had adored her, catered to her every whim and his search for their lost child had been unending.

The children worshipped their new nursemaid who they called Lucy. Gradually she filled the gap left in the household by their mother. Their home became a happy place full of fun and laughter although their activities were frequently confined to 'below stairs'. Lucy was very wary of her new employer for a number of reasons, mainly his right and ability to dismiss her at a moment's notice should he so desire. He was a moody and unhappy man who, at times, gave vent to a nasty temper. During such moments his voice would echo throughout every floor of the building. Invariably something would be smashed as it was pounded on the nearest surface to emphasise his wrath.

The two older children had reverted to calling Adolphe by the name used in the early days by their mother, Bebo, a diminutive of the Italian bambino. Lucy delighted in her new family although Wilfred sometimes seemed to nurture a particularly naughty streak and Daisy could be extremely petulant and, at times, withdrawn. But Bebo was her angel, her own perfect little boy. Lucy was his champion, his protector, his nurse and mother.

Bebo was nearly two and a half years old when, in July 1901, his travels recommenced due to his father being recalled to the head office in Constantinople.

The family set off in a small boat on the Tigris to complete the first stage of the journey at Kut-el-Amara, where a retinue of servants joined them with their luggage. The next stage was undertaken by caravan to Basra and the Persian Gulf. From there they embarked on a ship heading towards their new home by way of Aden and the Red Sea.

Arthur Cooper was making the most of a break in his usually busy routine. The voyage was leisurely and Lucy had been instructed to keep the children out of his way. Much of

11

his time was taken up with personal correspondence peppered by an occasional daydream. Arthur Cooper was a very lonely man, and these daydreams were becoming more frequent as the journey progressed.

Lucy was trying hard to keep the children from annoying their father but it was proving difficult to keep an eye on two active children and attend to young Bebo. One afternoon their tea was late, so she left her youngest charge in the apparent safety of the cabin and hurried off to enquire the reason for the delay.

Screams brought Lucy back to the cabin. Somehow, in her absence, the spirit stove had been upset. The girl ran through the smoke and flames, grabbed the child and threw him out onto the deck. The boy's clothes were scorched, his hair was singed but it was his back that had borne the main force of the flames. He was in agony for many weeks with severe burns. While Lucy blamed herself for the child's injuries, much to her horror the ship's crew and passengers all treated her as a heroine.

As the ship docked at Beirut, Arthur's loneliness and depression deepened, for this was where his mother lived. He was a proud man, the epitome of a Victorian father and he was bitter at Elenora's deceit and desertion. The force of his feelings intensified when the ship rounded Seraglio Point into the Golden Horn where spread before him was Constantinople, home of his friends and relations. The Coopers were a distinguished family with evidence of paternal ancestry dating back to 1641. Arthur's father had been taken to Constantinople after his death at Adrianople. The body was later buried alongside the British dead of the Crimean war in the Protestant Cemetery at Scutari, across the Bosphorus from the Turkish capital. His father was well known throughout Turkey and had been decorated by Sultan Abdul-Hamid with the Order of the Medjidie for his services to the Ottoman Empire.

The children took Constantinople by storm for they had been cooped up on a boat for far too long. Bebo had recovered from his burns and like any toddler was ready to explore and investigate. The mix of languages spoken by the children enthralled their relatives and friends; even the baby's childish chatter was a unique blend of Arabic, Turkish and English. Since their father spoke more than a dozen languages, Lucy could speak Arabic and Turkish, one maid spoke French and another Italian, their house was a veritable Tower of Babel. The three children would jabber away in a composite language of their own, unintelligible to outsiders. Anger would bring out the full glory of their linguistic skills as, red faced, they would search for phrases to express the feelings rushing up inside them. In the years to come they never felt the need to resort to profanities, as their vocabulary was more than sufficient to cover any eventuality!

Soon the trunks were repacked and the family travelled to the lovely island of Chios off the west coast of Asia Minor in the Aegean Sea, at that time part of the Ottoman Empire.

Their new home was a spacious self-contained apartment close to the harbour. Arthur was absorbed in his work, which frequently took him away from home for weeks on end, sometimes to the other islands and on occasions to Smyrna.

It was Lucy who ran the home, who organised their days and filled the house with laughter. They would explore the island, picnic at the water's edge and play thrilling games of make-believe until, exhausted at the end of their day, they would climb into their beds and Lucy would sing them a Greek lullaby.

They lived on Chios for almost two years, leaving in 1904 when Arthur was again recalled to Constantinople.

For young Bebo life had already held adventure but these first five years stood him in good stead, for the events that were to follow would test him to the limit, time and time again. Many years were to pass before Bebo would once again be as truly happy as he was during those blissful days on the lovely island of Chios.

A few months later the family was again on the move and sailed for Aleppo, in Syria. Lucy remained with the family but the other servants were all dismissed.

It was during the voyage that the children were introduced to their stepmother. Her presence came as a shock to them all for Arthur had never mentioned the woman, let alone his intention to marry again. Their new mother was the daughter of Berovitch Pasha, one of the Governors of Albania, then under Turkish control. She was a Christian, young, inexperienced and quite obviously jealous of Lucy and her place in the children's lives. In the days and weeks that followed Lucy was to find herself pushed further and further into the background by this tiny, arrogant young woman.

The boat put into Alexandretta, the most northerly of the Syrian ports which serviced Aleppo. The quay was unsuitable for large vessels and therefore passengers were forced to disembark into small boats by means of a rope ladder. This could be quite frightening for the inexperienced - men and women alike. The ladders were narrow and slippery, the seas choppy and the boats would bob up and down relentlessly. The voluminous dresses of the ladies only served to make the whole process more difficult. Five-year-old Bebo had none of these problems as he was seated in a box type swing and lowered by ropes.

While the family awaited a caravan for the next stage of the journey, they were to shelter within the safety of a caravanserai. This traveller's shelter from bandits and wolves was a small fortress of a number of rooms built around a large courtyard. A single entrance was guarded by heavy wooden double doors, which were locked and bolted throughout the night.

As they entered the quadrangle, the family was greeted by a deafening tumult of animal noises. An odd mixture of camels, horses and cows were stamping and barging in fear as hens fluttered and scurried between their hooves.

Bebo's face was a picture of sheer delight and, unable to contain his excitement, he wrenched his hand from the grasp of his new mother and leapt into the throng. Like most young children he adored animals and had no fear of them. Darting here and there he was stroking the quieter beasts and helping others to large handfuls of food. Then he made a big mistake, stopping to stroke a camel that was sitting ruminating, he was rewarded with an unpleasant deposit of cud on his best suit.

Looking down to survey the damage his surprise turned to shock as a blow to his face sent him flying across the compound. For the first time he was seeing his stepmother in her real colours. In fury she had hurled him into the dust at the feet of the animals.

The child was used to punishment and Lucy had often, unobtrusively, padded his trousers when he had run foul of his father. These had been cold and metered punishments, but this was a new experience, smouldering and vicious.

The little boy forced back the tears; even at his tender age he was determined not to show weakness in the face of the enemy. This woman was to be avoided at all costs, not that it would be easy for they were to stay two days in a large room curtained into three sleeping compartments.

When he felt it was safe, Bebo found Lucy and buried his head in her skirts. Still the child refused to give way to tears but Lucy could feel his shoulders shaking as she held him close.

The next day as the mistress reclined in her room, Lucy found herself playing a game of hide and seek as she looked for Bebo among the animals. The child was rushing around and darting through fur covered legs to evade his nurse. When they both tired of the game he would try to help the drovers harness the animals but was frequently knocked over as the men moved swiftly about their work.

Covered wagons, called arabas, were to carry them on the next stage of their journey. The Aleppo bound caravan was drawn up outside the caravanserai. Nearby were six dismounted Circassians or Tcherkess, originally from Caucasus, who were to form the bodyguard. They wore fluffy hats, long warm coats reaching down to the top of their leather boots, with daggers protruding from their breast pockets.

There was no direct route to Aleppo and they were to travel many more than the sixty-five miles which could be flown by crows. Most of the roads were unmade and in places particularly unsafe hence the need for protectors. The children were positioned in the safest place, on the floor of the wagon. Their father and stepmother were on seats that ran the length of the vehicle and Lucy sat next to the driver. Two horsemen rode in front, one on each flank and two bringing up the rear. The passengers hung on desperately as the arabas lurched forward at breakneck speed, the Circassian riders shouting 'Yalah, Yalah' as they whipped their galloping horses.

They were heading south to Top Borazi then northeast to Toun and Jenikol. On the first day they travelled more than fifty miles, the children bouncing up and down on the floor grabbing at each other and any likely anchor they could find, including their father's legs. Even in acute discomfort they knew better than to touch their new mother.

An overnight stop was made at Haman where exhaustion ensured that everyone slept well. The next day they took the northern route to Kersen and their guards were particularly watchful, as the area was known to harbour raiders. Many of the marauders were Kurds. At the turn of the century the Kurds were said to be among the best soldiers in the Turkish army but they were also considered the most formidable of bandits.

On the other hand the Circassians were renowned as fearless fighters.

With another seventy-five miles to go the journey took a total of three days to complete. They reached Kefer Miz without incident and then turned south towards Kefr-Naja. Although everyone, even the children, had been aware that an attack might come, when it did they were taken by surprise. Suddenly the sound of gunfire was deafening as riders were pounding towards them. The arabas stopped with a skid and the Circassians pulled them from the wagon and heaved them into the ditch, which conveniently bordered the road.

Pushing Bebo's enquiring head below ground level, Arthur began firing at the attackers. Their driver was also giving rapid covering fire. Meanwhile the Circassians had remounted their horses and, although heavily outnumbered, were riding directly towards their assailants firing their guns from the hip as they rode.

Lucy was shielding the children. Daisy and Wilfred were old enough to be terrified by the experience but young Bebo continually raised his head to see what was happening. It was only later when the child constantly recalled the event that it became evident he had been deeply affected by the incident.

The skirmish had continued for some time and it was the timely arrival of some friendly horsemen who, hearing the shots, had galloped to their rescue. When they arrived safely in Aleppo the following day, it was a relief to them all.

Their new home was a six-roomed furnished apartment with an extensive kitchen and the luxury of a bathroom, rare in those parts. Two balconies overlooked a bazaar and below, to the left, was their own spacious courtyard. Farez, who had been with them in Baghdad, opened the door with a welcoming smile. Farez was now alone. His wife, who had been responsible for so many heartaches, had died suddenly of food poisoning.

It was time for Bebo to start school. It was hardly surprising that he was already a rebellious child. Family rules were harsh and at five years of age the boy was used to gritting his teeth in defiance while punishment was metered out in fairly large doses. The seed of restlessness had long since been implanted in his soul by Hassan and Lucy. Even with his family he had lived the life of a Nomad never knowing any restriction of movement. He was like a runaway train on a blocked line and school was one obstacle to be met head-on.

There was no introduction to school life, no playschool or nursery to help prepare him. His stepmother's interest was limited to getting rid of him for long periods. Lucy, knowing nothing of schools, wholeheartedly disapproved of his unnecessary removal from her tender care. Knowing that Lucy was unhappy only served to frighten the child and he fought like a demon to stay with her.

The infant school had an excellent reputation within the European community of Aleppo; it was run by the Sisters of Charity of the Order of St. Vincent de Paul. Daisy and Bebo started the school together. His sister was quiet and introverted, deeply affected by the disappearance of her real mother so that school offered a haven, a distraction from her unhappiness. For young Bebo things were a little different, his mischievous sense of humour was bound to get him into trouble. To his horror he was put into a class of precocious girls who set about making his life a misery. In a misguided attempt at retaliation the boy pinched one of his tormentors good and hard on her backside. And so it was within a very short time of starting school that Bebo was given several strokes of the ruler on his hand, a trend that was going to continue with increasing severity.

No caring parent would wish this introduction to school on any child and one could quite easily predict the outcome. A few months later Arthur was summoned to the school and asked to remove his youngest son as his mischief making was disruptive and he was a bad influence on the other children. Sadly the Sisters were seriously lacking when it came to being 'Charitable.' Lucy duly padded the trousers of her headstrong young charge before taking him, with great reluctance, to his father's study where his punishment was, yet again, dispensed with the stick.

Very soon young Bebo took to creeping away from the house to play with the children of Arabs, Turks and Jews. The old city of Aleppo was a hive of activity where real life excitement was to be found in the bazaars. Often Lucy would be forced to seek him out, cleaning the dust from his hair and clothing before his hawkeyed stepmother saw him.

In most Turkish and Arab towns there were numerous stray mongrel dogs, unloved and unwanted scavengers. Aleppo was no exception and a gang of children set upon one of these animals kicking and stoning the half-starved wretch. No doubt it was the sympathy of a fellow sufferer that motivated Bebo. Grabbing a broom handle he waded in hitting out at everyone and everything in sight in an effort to protect the terrified dog. He continued lashing out even as shopkeepers tried to intervene.

It took the weight and authority of a Turkish policeman to break up the fracas. He seized the little tornado by the scruff of his neck and dragged him off to the police station. A number of particularly unsavoury characters viewed the new inmate with interest and one old Arab woman decided to mother him. Bebo was well practised in hiding fear but this situation took considerable effort. When he was handed a cigarette he smoked away with a poise belied only by the tears in his eyes and the green tinge to his face.

Nowhere was corruption rifer than at the local police station and it was reasonably simple for Lucy and Farez to pay for the child's instant release. Lucy had dipped into her meagre savings to pay the bribe as soon as news had reached her of the boy's incarceration. Luckily they managed to keep this latest escapade from Arthur.

School was not to be avoided and so arrangements were made for Bebo to join Wilfred at an establishment run by the Jesuits. The Jesuit Brothers were said to be good teachers if somewhat strict. Bound to poverty, chastity and obedience they appeared determined to extract the same obedience from their charges. Sadly the rigorous training of the Brothers had excluded forgiveness and mercy.

Unlike the casual and relaxed atmosphere enjoyed in modern infant departments so familiar to our offspring, the Jesuit Brothers did not allow talking in the classroom. For Bebo, this was an impossibility; his zest for life had nurtured an inquiring mind and an active tongue. Punishment was severe and cruel. The child was made to kneel on rice so that gradually the seed would eat into the flesh causing excruciating pain. Only when the little beads of blood appeared was he allowed to resume his seat, knees bent with cramp and pain making every step an agonising effort. For one so little he was already extremely tough and would exasperate the Brothers with his calm acceptance of their methods, the jaunty upward tilt of his chin and the mischievous twinkle in his eye.

Home was no better than school and although he tried to avoid his stepmother he was constantly falling foul of her. There was an occasion when he was caught taking one of the many bunches of grapes piled high upon a tray in the kitchen. His stepmother barred his way and when he tried to dodge round her she lunged forward to hit him, he grabbed her arm to save himself and then bit into her flesh with his baby teeth as hard as he could.

The woman screamed and swooned, just as one would expect of a lady of her time and standing. Being completely innocent of female wiles, the youngster ran for his life. God knows what his father would do this time! Never had he been so frightened. He ran on and on turning corner after corner until he reached the edge of town. A caravan was preparing to leave and he attempted to stowaway but was seen and sent on his way.

Slowly retracing his steps he saw one of the Sisters from his first school. The child's distress was there for all to see and so the Sister took him by the hand and persuaded him to confess his sins. Hearing his garbled account of the recent events the teacher led him home where she spoke to his father in the privacy of the study.

On this occasion he was not given the usual flogging by Arthur but was taken to the study where they had a heart to heart. At least that was Arthur's description of their meeting. Bebo had climbed up on to the dark brown leather chair and peered red eyed at his father. The child's face was ashen and his little legs stuck out at attention from the seat of the studded chair.

After a barrage of standard questions from the man and tearful disjointed answers from the child came his father's final query, "Don't you love us?"

Candid as only a child can be he replied, "Not very much. I only love Lucy."

"In that case there is only one thing to do," said his father. "If you continue with your atrocious behaviour, Lucy will have to go."

His world rocked on its very axis. Lucy was the only mother the child had known, the person who protected him as only a mother will protect her young. Bebo was only six years old and his father's ultimatum was the cruellest blow yet. The boy had learned to live with physical cruelty, but mental cruelty was far beyond the understanding of his years. In a few well-chosen words his father had shattered the fragment of stability that had held his world together. If Lucy could be dismissed from his life so easily then he was without hope or refuge.

For the first time in years the boy began to cry unrestrainedly in front of his father. Lucy rushed in without so much as by your leave and carried him to her room, tears streaming down her own cheeks. Between sobs he told her all his father had said, adding that he would try his very hardest to be good. He made her promise faithfully that she would never leave without him and finally he fell asleep in her arms his young body giving an occasional fitful shudder as he slept.

2 Bereaved

The children's stepmother was expecting her first child but this apparently welcome news did nothing to improve the woman's disposition. The only advantage to be gained from her condition was her tendency to spend long hours in her rooms. The birth of Hetty in August 1905 caused hardly a stir in the nursery as the new baby was kept well away from the children and from Lucy.

For a wonderful six months life was bearable once again as Bebo's stepmother had completely lost interest in him, while the bond between Lucy and Arthur's children strengthened with each passing day. In appearance, Daisy and Bebo were very much like their natural mother having inherited her dark hair and thick eyebrows whereas Wilfred was fairer skinned with lighter shades in his hair. Had it not been for their European clothing the two younger children could have easily been mistaken as Lucy's own family. The Moroccan nursemaid was a very beautiful young woman, her dark features being complemented by the whiteness of her traditionally styled dress and head-dress.

Their happy days came to an abrupt end when once again Arthur was summoned to Constantinople en route for yet another transfer. It was early in 1906 when the family journeyed to Beirut by caravan via Hama and Homs. A grand family reunion awaited them in Beirut and for several days the children were pinched, poked and prodded affectionately by a variety of admiring relations including their grandmother. Bebo was now fluent in seven languages. It was only in the eighth, English, that he had a slight indefinable accent.

Much to the relief of the little ones they sailed within the week and the voyage was memorable for the sheer beauty of the region. They entered the Sea of Marmara with the Dardanelles to their left heading towards the Bosphorus and the magnificence of Constantinople. There was a heat haze just above the water as they sailed between the lands of Europe and Asia Minor towards the seven hills of Constantinople.

Rounding the point into the Golden Horn the splendour of a waterside Mosque towering above a marketplace in the old town took Bebo's breath away. The vessel was heading towards the right bank and the new town area of Galata. This was the quarter favoured by the rich, particularly by rich Europeans. It was luxurious and very expensive. The apartments placed at Arthur's disposal were actually owned by a Turkish Pasha who was a friend of the Cooper family.

Arrangements were made for the children to attend local schools as Arthur had finally decided to resign his post, disheartened by the numerous transfers, endless travels and a wife who constantly nagged for a permanent home.

Daisy was sent to an Armenian Catholic Convent and the two boys were packed off to the College of St Joseph at Kadikeui. Although the ancient Chalcedon of Kadikeui was easily reached by boat, arrangements were made for the boys to become boarders at the Jesuit school.

Any child attending boarding school for the first time is bound to be apprehensive. They may be looking forward to the experience, may even by excited at the prospect, but will inevitably be nervous of the unknown. Bebo had lived the life of a wanderer and there was nowhere the seven year old could identify as home, except that wherever Lucy was to be found, was his home. His brother being with him was no comfort for Wilf was equally distressed. Would their father move again in their absence? If that happened, how would they find Lucy? Their mother had gone away; she had left them and never returned!

Two frightened little boys crossed the Bosphorus by ferry under the watchful eye of a stern faced housemaster, sent to collect the new pupils and their trunks of clothes.

Meanwhile Arthur had applied for, and obtained, a lucrative position with a newly formed company. The Turkish Government had awarded a major irrigation contract to the French and the Entreprise Generale d'Irrigation Laporte was formed by a Monsieur Laporte. Arthur Cooper was appointed the chief accountant with the title Chef Comptable de la Compagnie.

The children's fears were well founded for Arthur and his new family were to live in Tchoumra (Cumra), some three hundred miles away from Constantinople, where canalisation was to start. Water was to be taken from three lakes: Kureli Golu, Egridir Golu and Sogla Golu.

To travel to that area from Constantinople was to be transported to another world. Just twenty-five miles from Tchoumra was the town of Konia, home of the Whirling Dervishes. This was a cold and desolate region laying 3320 feet above sea level and suffering from a water shortage, aggravated by heavy concentrations of salt in the soil. Wolves, jackals and hyenas roamed the countryside and frequently caused havoc in night time raids on the tiny isolated villages.

This was the place to which Bebo's father took his new wife, his younger daughter and Lucy. Farez was no longer to be with them. By mutual consent and with a small gratuity he settled in Konia.

The Entreprise Laporte had built a small village of single storey houses for their senior employees. The settlement was close to Tchoumra and a palisade offered protection from the outside world.

The gangs of labourers - Turks, Kurds, Armenians and Arabs - lived close to the work site under canvas just as their forefathers had done for hundreds of years. There were no bulldozers or other mechanical aids to speed the excavations. These men worked with picks and shovels.

While Arthur settled his little family happily into their new lifestyle, Bebo was not faring so well. Adjustment at school was difficult. By now he knew his family had gone away and he was unable to settle to anything. Routine was not something that he recognised and he could work up no enthusiasm for children's games. Instead he would scale the wall and spend his time with the ragged Turkish children in their quarter of Kadikeui. These were moments he could relate to the old days in Aleppo when his family was together.

It was inevitable that the boy would be caught and when the Brothers finally tired of his activities, he was severely punished. Sent to his dormitory, Bebo faced two of the Brothers armed with a towel and a basin of water. The child was told to drop his trousers and was then unmercifully lashed across bare buttocks with the wet towel. Meanwhile a letter was sent to Arthur advising him that his son would be expelled the very next time he misbehaved.

A cholera epidemic was sweeping through Turkey killing many people. The boys were warned not to have contact with anyone outside the school. The young children were given to understand that only the school and the European community would be safe.

There were lurid tales of people dropping dead in the streets and of Turkish patrols soaking the bodies with paraffin and setting fire to them where they lay. Bebo was distraught; he had to know if the stories were true. Lucy was on the outside and she was a Moroccan.

Waiting until his classmates were settled in their beds, he dressed quickly and quietly and went over the school wall. Kadikeui was deserted. Nothing stirred except mangy dogs roaming in packs. Any stray dog wandering into the path of these vicious scavengers faced death.

Seeing no evidence of funeral pyres and no human corpses, the boy decided to return to his bed. As he turned to retrace his steps, a frenzied mass of dogs tore along the street to attack a mongrel puppy. Without thought for his own safety, Bebo plunged into the affray and snatching the puppy from the jaws of certain death he received a savage bite on his leg. Clutching the puppy, he climbed up to sit astride the school wall with the yelps of the cheated dogs ringing in his ears.

Examining the animal, Bebo found its creamy coat splashed with blood from a number of minor wounds. The puppy snuggled close to his rescuer, licking the hand that stroked him as instinct told him he had found a friend at last.

Compared with the problems ahead, saving the dog had been easy. The boy knew that he was now personally responsible for the tiny creature's life. What could he do? Then he remembered old Garcia, the school gardener.

Garcia was a Sephardi Jew, whose peoples had lived in Spain until they were driven out in the fifteenth century by the inquisition. As Bebo was the only other person in the school to speak Spanish, the language of Garcia's ancestors, a close bond had grown between man and boy.

The gardener lived in a small hut in the school grounds, sleeping alongside the tools of his trade. He had many acres of ground to look after but always found time to tell his young friend of his experiences. The boy was sure he could rely on Garcia to help him care for the stray. He raced across the grounds, darted through a small clump of trees and arrived breathless at the door of the hut. Roused from his slumbers, the gardener managed to give a sympathetic ear to Bebo's story. Although he knew he was risking his job, he agreed to keep the dog.

It was long after midnight when the boy crept to his bed, thankful his absence had gone unnoticed. He lay awake, gazing at the uneven ceiling, making plans. His need for the dog was equal only to the animal's need of him. As his eyes closed, Bebo decided to call his furry young friend Osman (Turk).

A few days later a letter arrived from Lucy, obviously written for her by a Turkish public writer, in which she gave the address of Farez in Konia. The letter begged young Bebo to write to her care of Farez as she was very concerned, having heard whispers of his various escapades. The boy treasured the letter and slept with it under his pillow until he suddenly realised that, if found, it could bring nothing but harm to both of them. Reluctantly he destroyed his only link with Lucy.

Osman immediately recognised his rescuer when Bebo visited him the following day. Old Garcia could not provide the animal with food and so the boy ate less at meal times, pocketing half his bread and other titbits from the refectory table. During meal times he was absorbed by his latest task, effecting sleight of hand. The pockets of his uniform became gunged with squashed food and he was forced to wash them out under the tap. Matron must never suspect his secret and he was certainly not going to tell any of the boys.

A second letter arrived from Lucy and as he read her news he was over the moon with excitement. She wrote that she was leaving her employment with his father and travelling to Kadikeui to be near him. It was to be their secret and hopefully she would find suitable work close to the school.

Lucy was to arrive on the Saturday and Bebo would see her the following day. The hours dragged by until Sunday finally dawned and his feet floated on air as he raced to meet his 'adopted' mother. In his haste he almost forgot Osman who was skipping and jumping at his side.

Close to the lighthouse of Fanaraki stood a pretty Turkish house with green shutters and a trim little garden surrounded by a low white wall. There, in that garden, stood Lucy. As he reached her, Bebo was swept into her arms and hugged until he was breathless. Words tumbled out making little sense except to express the joy of their meeting. The boy was due back at school for Sunday lunch and he left her happily, safe in the knowledge that she was near and that he was to return in the afternoon. Osman was left in Lucy's safe-keeping and it was a contented child who turned and gaily waved to his loved ones as he made his way back to the school.

It was necessary to fool the school nurse into believing he was sick and unable to take part in the usual Sunday afternoon walk in the company of the Brothers. He was becoming very adept in the art of escape and evasion and found little difficulty in feigning illness. As soon as the coast was clear he was up and away, heading back towards the lighthouse and Lucy.

Exchanging news, Bebo heard how Lucy had left his father's house in the early hours of the morning without so much as a word. A horse drawn araba had taken her to Konia where she had met Farez. The kindly man had lent her some money and sent her on her way by train to the famous Haidar-Pasha terminus close to Kadikeui.

The ever enterprising Lucy managed to obtain paid employment in the school laundry giving her the chance to keep an eye on Bebo while earning the money for her rent.

Together once again, the woman and child felt their happiness to be impregnable, particularly as there was no sign of Arthur and his lady wife. Sadly their joy was to be very short lived as destiny was about to deal a fatal hand. The first sign of a change in fortune came in the form of an edict by the Turkish Government: - All Stray Dogs Were To Be Destroyed.

Osman had never shaken the habit of wandering off on his own and so Bebo, Lucy and Garcia made a concerted effort to train him. They spent hours teaching him to recognise a special whistle and to obey their orders. Nevertheless the day came when he was caught in the daily round up of stray dogs.

Lucy tried as hard as she could to trace the vehicle that would carry Osman to his fate. Vans would take the animals to Haidar Pasha where boats would be waiting at the quayside to transport the strays to the Princes Islands in the Sea of Marmara. These islands may now be popular holiday resorts but not in 1907. The dogs were dropped on to one of the smaller islands called Oxyaea, a stretch of barren land used as a canine graveyard. There was nothing humane about the system; the dogs were simply left to die of hunger and thirst.

That night Bebo lay awake for hours trying to think of a way to save Osman. There seemed to be only one solution - to take a boat to the island. He was confident that Osman would swim out to him when he heard their special whistle but first he must enlist the help of Lucy and Garcia!

On Sunday, the day chosen for the rescue attempt, Bebo left school before breakfast knowing full well that he would be reported missing and consequently expelled. Garcia went with him to meet Lucy and although he obviously thought it a foolhardy venture he made no attempt to stop it. An araba carried them from Kadikeui to Kartal, a small village facing the Princes Islands and offering the shortest route. They had no trouble hiring a boat, a thirteen-foot Turkish caique, typical of the many inshore craft to be seen in those waters.

They did not want to run foul of the police, so they waited until dusk before pushing the boat out into the waves. "Allah help us", murmured Lucy. She too made no attempt to stop the daring mission. A clammy feeling of danger swept over the boy as the breeze stiffened.

It was the moment when an eight-year-old boy needed adult confirmation that he was indeed wrong, a time when a gentle and loving explanation was required, an explanation of the fact that he could not save his dog. Both Lucy and Garcia were simple folk but that could not excuse their irresponsible behaviour in allowing the child to continue in such a wild pursuit.

Moonlight helped confirm what their progress had already told them - strong currents were running parallel to the coast, like smooth, swift flowing rivers in the sea.

It would have been eerie enough without the spine chilling howls of maddened dogs they could hear in the distance. The noise, gushing suddenly louder in the wind, was like that of a thousand ravenous wolves. Intermingled with this were the distinct sounds of fighting, as if the dogs were killing each other. Only then did the inexperienced liberators realise that the whistle of a small boy would not be heard in such a din.

In this macabre setting was played out the most painful tragedy in the boy's life. Garcia was attempting to turn the sail when a gust of wind caught it. A spar whipped across the boat knocking Bebo into the sea where he was caught in a strong current. Lucy, hearing him yell out as he went over the side, shouted at Garcia and then plunged fully clothed after the child. For a moment she had hold of his collar but the seas wrenched him from her grasp.

Time and time again the boy went under and he was more dead than alive when Garcia finally reached him. The man had swung the boat around, secured a rope and leapt into the sea, hanging on to the rope as a lifeline. Somehow Garcia managed to tie the line around the boy, struggling back, hand over fist, to the side of the boat. Bebo was unconscious and the man had to use superhuman effort to get himself and the child back on board.

Slowly regaining consciousness, Bebo reached out for Lucy. With tears in his eyes, Garcia said "I am sorry. She was lost in the waves and you were closer."

Frantic with grief the child tried to leap back into the sea. He had to find her! The man grappled with him, forcing him to the bottom of the boat. Bebo screamed and struggled until he was forcibly tied with the rope used earlier to rescue him.

Garcia made no attempt to hide the disaster, reporting all the facts to the police when they finally made it back to Kartal. The day, which had started in a lively spirit of bravado, ended with man and boy in police custody weeping in each other's arms.

The full significance of what had happened began to dawn on the child. Lucy was no more. The world he had built around her was shattered. It was his fault, he had killed her, he knew he had killed her and now he just wanted to die. He was inconsolable.

Eventually, seeking some relief from his agony of guilt, he began to think of the religious teachings of the Brothers. They had said the soul is immortal and he fervently prayed that they were right. He made up his mind that someone as wonderful as Lucy would be among the archangels. Lucy was there, she would watch over him. Again and again he prayed, asking Lucy to stay near him forever.

There were to be many times in the future when he believed that his simple prayers in a Kartal police cell were answered. Many times when danger struck he was aware of Lucy at his side.

Eventually two Brothers arrived in a carriage to take him back to the school. Seeing them, he rushed to Garcia and, with his arms around the man's neck, cried, "I am sorry! I have ruined everyone's life. I wish I were dead."

It must have been two or three in the morning when they arrived back at the school. Bebo was thrust into a small room and the door was locked firmly behind him. He lay dry eyed on the hard, uninviting bed, spending the rest of the night gazing into space awaiting the morning that would dawn without Lucy.

Daylight was streaming into the room before anyone came near him. A cup of bitter coffee was brought to him by a silent Brother. The silence was to continue for three whole days. They fed and watered the child and that was all. Perhaps they intended it, not as a punishment, but a period of self-examination. But the child was only eight years old. Self-torture was all they could achieve from such inhumanity.

The wall of silence was breached when his brother was allowed to see him. They were left alone in the locked cell and immediately Wilf tackled him about Lucy's job in the laundry, wanting to know why they had not confided in him.

"I hoped you would not find out," Bebo told him. "You would have told father if you had known."

"They have telegraphed father and he is arriving this afternoon to take you away." Wilf stood looking down at the floor for a moment, then wished his young brother the best of luck. He was about to leave when suddenly he turned back and gave Bebo a quick hug and kiss. Bebo stood looking bemused as Wilf rapped the door indicating that he wished to leave.

When his father arrived, the man was stern-faced and unspeaking. He went to see the school director while the boy's belongings were packed. When the time came to leave, Arthur turned to Wilf and said, "Say goodbye to your brother. I don't know when you will see him again."

The dejected child rallied as they were passing the director's office and, on impulse, he brushed past them and burst into the room. Facing the director across a wide expanse of desk top Bebo asked, "What will happen to Garcia?"

"He will rot in jail," came the answer, harsh and to the point.

"Call yourselves Christians?" shouted Bebo. "Garcia is a Jew and a thousand times better than you. From now on Jews will be my friends. I hate Christians. I will not be a Christian!"

"Sacrilege, sacrilege," said the director as he and all Brothers in earshot bowed their heads and crossed themselves.

The Journey to the irrigation company's village at Tchoumra was like that of a prisoner under escort. They drove by carriage to the Haidar-Pasha railway station where Bebo was locked in a room at the station hotel for the night. Early the next morning they boarded the Tchoumra bound train. They sat facing each other, his father maintaining a taciturn mood and refusing to discuss either the past or the future. That was the way they were to remain for the best part of three days. Two brooding figures looking out of train windows.

From his window the child saw Iznit Ortakeui before Eskischir, their overnight stop, loomed out of the gathering dusk. All passengers disembarked and went to a hotel because the trains then serving Asia Minor did not run at night.

They had a second overnight stop, this time at Aksehir, the next day passing through Konia. It was late at night when they finally arrived home in Tchoumra. It was the evening of the next day before Arthur summoned the child to appear before him in the drawing room.

Standing before the man was an eight-year-old who was desperately in need of comfort and understanding. He was unlikely to be consoled, or to believe in his own innocence, but words of gentle logic might have given him a small degree of strength in the days to come. To be held and to be loved were the very basic needs of the child.

Arthur stared down at the lonely boy, a picture of sadness and dejection. He saw the hopelessness in the child's face and a hint of fear lurking behind the dark brown eyes that were rimmed in red. For a single moment there was a flicker of compassion in the man's face but then he recognised the mother in the face of the child. Elenora had betrayed him and so had her son!

"You are wondering why you have not been severely punished," his father began. "You seem to have been punished enough, as it is you will carry the guilt of Lucy's death with you for the rest of your life."

3 Cornered

For several days the child remained in his room until it was decided he would attend the Jenanian College in Konia.

He was met at Konia railway station by Monsieur Soulier, the owner of the most luxurious hotel in the area. If it was possible, Bebo became even more subdued as they entered the plush foyer of the hotel. Armchairs covered in silk damask were almost strewn across the wide expanse of marbled floor. A broad staircase curled its way to the elegant bedrooms, one of which was to offer Bebo shelter for the night. Left alone at last he stood on tiptoe to look out of the large window and was just able to make out the tree lined square that lay below. Eventually he forced himself into the double bed that stood almost central in the spacious room. The child felt very, very, small. Indeed, the child was very, very, small.

Mr. Jenanian, the director of his new school, was an American Armenian. The first surprise was the man's informality. He had an air of benevolence about him and he spoke French with an American accent.

For such an establishment to exist in 1907 was surprising as its free expression was more suited to the later part of the twentieth century. The gates were left wide open and, when not in class, the boy's lives were their own. They were encouraged to choose their own beds in whichever room they fancied. They even looked after their own clothing. Any restrictions on their out of class activities came from within their own ranks as the senior boys were expected to keep an eye on the younger pupils.

It was like nectar to Bebo after the schools of Aleppo and Kadikeui. The result was a surfeit of freedom which very quickly lost its lustre. What was the point of struggling over a wall and running away into town when the school gates were open anyway? This, of course, was precisely the reasoning behind Mr. Jenanian's method of teaching. It won Bebo over completely and for the first time he worked hard at his lessons, achieving more in a few months than he had in the previous two years.

The child tried his hardest to fit into school life, not that he stopped his trips of exploration. Konia, the Iconium of Biblical times, was a biggish town that was rising in prosperity after a downward plunge. Here, where St. Paul once preached, was the headquarters of the Mevlevi dervishes, the Mohammedan friars. Mendicant dervishes, in flowing robes topped by tall fezzes were a familiar sight on the roads of Asia Minor. Bebo got to know some of these in Konia and one or two became his firm friends.

When lessons were over he would leave the school by the main gate, cross the road and enter the cemetery by the rear gate. Row upon row of headstones stood in white relief against the dark green cypress trees and it was there he felt close to Lucy. Sometimes he would wonder about the Turkish custom of planting a tree for the dead. Should he plant a tree for Lucy? As far as he was aware her body had never been found.

One day as he wandered through the vast cemetery towards the town, Bebo heard a noise and seeking the source he came across a Dervish. "What are you doing?" questioned the child.

"Aksham manazi (evening devotions)," the man replied. Reading from the Koran, he explained the meaning of various passages to Bebo.

It sounded, to young ears, much more interesting than the Old and New Testaments and a lot more credible. Each evening after that he met with the Dervish in the cemetery and was guided through the regular postures, learning the words to recite in each position, kneeling, kissing the ground, and so on.

He began to learn the Koran in its original language, then, becoming uncertain with the wisdom of a full eight years behind him, he decided to seek out his own religion. In one thing his faith was unshakeable. He was certain there was life after death.

The child within him would surface when, on stolen visits to town, he gazed upon the variety of delicacies in the open fronted shops. Lack of money was a draw back for there were no doting relatives to spoil him with even the smallest treat. Now was as good a time as any to start living by his wits and so he started selling his books and items of his clothing to raise money for anything that took his fancy.

Bebo was relatively happy with his way of life, literally living for the moment until the holidays loomed on the horizon. Then he realised, with horror, that the clothes would be missed. As Christmas drew nearer the child existed in a constant state of terror. To go home with a half empty trunk was to openly invite his father's anger.

Inwardly shaking he climbed to the top of the school wall where he sat musing while watching his schoolmates at play. A sudden noise caught his attention and he turned to find a woman smiling up at him. "Sabah laher olsun (good morning)," he called.

"Do you want tea?" she asked.

No second invitation was needed. The boy jumped down,

took the bucket of water she had been carrying and followed his new found friend across a pretty courtyard.

Placing the bucket outside the open door the child entered a large room arranged in Arab style. The floor was carpeted; there were no chairs but cushions set against the walls offered comfort. Watching the child take in each small detail of the room, the woman explained that she was a Kurd but her husband was an Arab from Baghdad.

"I am from Baghdad," the child spoke with pride, straightening his shoulders as he squatted cross-legged on the floor. Bebo felt at home as he sipped the milkless tea but suddenly he was transfixed, rigid. He could feel the hairs at the back of his neck standing to attention. He had heard a voice drifting softly into the room from the courtyard.

Leaping to his feet, the boy almost head-butted his newly found friend in his anxiety to reach the courtyard and the owner of the voice. "Farez," he screamed. "Farez, Farez!" Tears were streaming down his cheeks as he raced to the safety of the man's arms.

Sometime after they had untangled themselves Bebo told the old retainer about Lucy's death. For the first time the child was able to unburden a little of the hell he had carried alone so bravely. As Farez cried for the loss of his dear friend Lucy, his wife was weeping for the boy and the torment in his eyes.

Each day Bebo would visit Farez and his second wife in their tiny home behind the school. It was there that they hatched a plan to deceive the boy's father in the matter of the missing clothing. Farez promised to replace the clothes and Bebo was to tell his father that a fire had destroyed the items and they had been replaced by the school. It sounded plausible but Bebo was such a candid child that he harboured doubts as to the success of the plan.

Meanwhile, Farez provided the ultimate distraction in the

form of 'Baku', a beautiful dog to replace Osman. The boy planned to take Baku home with him for the Christmas holidays.

Monsieur Soulier accompanied the boy and his dog to the station and would be responsible for sending the fateful trunk a few days later.

Arthur was in a relatively amiable mood when his youngest son arrived tired and dishevelled on the doorstep. Gazing at the boisterous dog yanking on a frayed piece of rope, Arthur agreed the animal could stay providing he was clean. "The first time he dirties, then out he goes," he said. Smiling hesitantly at his father, Bebo decided that his luck was changing for the better and for a short time he forgot about the trunk.

With his father's ultimatum clear in his mind, the boy rose early the next morning to take Baku for a run in the snow covered countryside. The high plains were in the grip of the Asia Minor winter with snow waist high in places.

A few days later the time-bomb, in the guise of his trunk, was delivered to the front door by a wizened railway porter.

"What is this?" demanded his stepmother, holding up a single item of his new clothes.

"It was a fire," the child mumbled feebly forgetting every word he had so carefully rehearsed. That evening he cracked completely under cross-examination by his father. The truth was the only way out.

"You will get it this time," Arthur threatened his son while indicating to his smiling wife that he wanted his stick.

Not again! Please God, not again! The child darted around his father and pushed past his stepmother. With one leap he was out of the front door and running for his life. Baku was bounding at his side and together they were off into the darkness towards the deserted plains. The moon reflected an eerie light on the snow and looking back, Bebo realised that the animated figure silhouetted against the whiteness was none other than his outraged father.

Eventually, knowing he would not be caught, Bebo crossed a couple of irrigation canals and slowed down. Only then did the child begin to notice the cold. Baku was fine in his shaggy coat but the boy turned on his heel and peered longingly towards the village lights. No! He was determined he would never go back. He would sooner die, frozen in the snow, before meeting the violence of his father again and the contempt of his stepmother.

Something was moving. A small dark shape was creeping towards him. As he peered into the blackness, there was a snarling noise coming from his right-hand side. "Quiet Baku," he whispered. Looking down he realised that Baku was close at his side and although his teeth were bared, he was silent. A large black patch appeared directly in front of them moving rapidly. Suddenly, as the dark shadow fragmented, Bebo realised they were facing a pack of wolves.

For a moment he stood calmly counting and had got to nine before the blood-curdling cries finally penetrated his mind. "Lucy, Lucy help us!" As he prayed the wolves appeared to hesitate and the child was sure he saw Lucy trying to shoo them away. Gaining strength from Lucy's presence he spoke to the animals. "Go away, good boys, go on and go away!"

It did not work. The wolves were circling, moving in for the kill. Baku darted side to side snapping in a valiant attempt to push back their attackers. Eventually the dog became trapped as he bravely tried to press home an attack. Four of the pack jumped on the dog and his throat was ripped from his body as the child looked on in horror.

Stealing himself to the same fate as his dog, Bebo could once again see Lucy standing between him and his attackers. Taking a step towards her, he realised that rapid rifle fire could be heard above the sound of horses galloping. The riders were almost on top of him when he was grabbed by the seat of his pants and thrown across the saddle of a charging steed.

His rescuers were Circassians, compatriots of the horsemen who had saved the family on the road to Aleppo. The wolves re-grouped to attack the horses but, yet again, the Circassians opened fire. As they rode from the scene of the bloodbath, a bullet was put into Baku to ensure his suffering was ended.

Although Bebo's father had initiated the rescue, the child was not taken home but deposited instead at the local police station.

There were no Christmas celebrations for the youngster who spent the next two days in custody. Certainly the Circassians and the policemen made every effort to show kindness to such a small captive. With vivid memories of Lucy, Osman and Baku, the boy was inconsolable.

According to the latest instructions of his father, Bebo was given a change of clothing and put on a train for Constantinople. As the journey progressed, the child gazed at memories mirrored in the window of the train. He saw the smiling face of Farez and his kindly new wife. For a while he watched his brother and sister playing on the beaches of Chios. Then, once again, he prayed with his Dervish friend in the cemetery at Konia. They prayed for Lucy, for Osman, Baku and for a good friend, Garcia.

Apparently, Arthur had enlisted his employer's support in dealing with his wayward son. Bebo was met at Galata by Mr. Moraitis, the agent for Entreprise Laporte. The following day the boy was delivered to the offices of his family's solicitor, Edwin Pears.

"What ails you boy? I have known your grandfather and father for many years."

The man spoke in the voice of a prosecuting counsel. "Why can't you settle down like any other ordinary child, behave yourself and be a good son?"

These were questions the child could not begin to answer. Perhaps the eminent solicitor was unaware of the traumatic events in the life of one so young. If so, then the man was not qualified to make any judgements.

Experience had made the child a fatalist and so he waited silently for the latest proclamation. Apparently a complete change of surroundings was considered once again to be in his best interest and the route to a settled way of life. This time he was to stay in Constantinople with an aunt and uncle.

In the early weeks, with the stuffing still knocked out of him, the scheme appeared to work reasonably well. Bebo was sent to the school of St. John the Baptist, only a few minutes away from home. The family was good to him and he repaid the kindnesses by studying hard and leading a more or less sedentary life.

No matter how good his intentions, they were destined for destruction as he was caught up in a whirlpool of events. This time it was a revolution that intruded, without invitation, into his young life.

Bebo was now nine years old. It was 1908 and the Young Turks of the Union of the Progress Party made their big effort to free the country of the Abdul-Hamid regime. In July of that year an armed uprising at Resna was the spark that sent the flames of revolt sweeping through the empire.

In Constantinople, Bebo was making his way to school as usual when he became embroiled with the Young Turks running through the streets. There was a heady whiff of patriotism in the air as the young men charged on shouting, "Cheers for Liberty, Fraternity, Equality." Caught up in the hysteria of the moment, Bebo found himself in the midst of the charging mob, yelling the motto for all he was worth.

The atmosphere of rebellion was intoxicating. Bullets whistled all around, unnoticed - except by those who fell. The main charge turned the corner of Marango Sokak into the Grande Rue de Pera, the city's principal street. It was here that Bebo fell with a bullet in his thigh. It was as though someone had whacked him in the leg with a stake. Looking down he saw the hole in his trousers and the blood trickling down his leg.

Sobering, his first thought was of his unexplained absence from the classroom. Even getting involved in a revolution was not an acceptable excuse for being late. As he limped towards the school the pain gradually overtook the initial numbness of shock and he collapsed on to a doorstep. Forcing himself to stand again, he called out to an elderly woman and showed her the wound. Minutes later the school director was summoned and arriving out of breath, the man struggled to carry the boy to the French Hospital for treatment.

The wound was not too serious so although Arthur had been notified of the incident, he chose not to visit his son. When the time came to return to his lessons, Bebo was sent to an Italian school. The child was grateful for the opportunity to learn to write the language of the mother he had never known, a language he could speak fluently.

Arthur raised no objections to Bebo becoming a boarder at the Collegio Bartolomeo Giustiniani, the only Italian school in Constantinople. Run by the Salesian Fathers, the school was close to the Square of Liberty.

Life took a distinct turn for the better. Discipline at the school was strict but scrupulously fair. This was something understood and appreciated by the pupils. It was here, for a few short years, that Bebo found sanctuary. Here he was treated with compassion and understanding. The Director and his staff genuinely wanted to help the boy. Bebo was questioned gently about many aspects of his young life as they sought the reasons for his obvious resentment of authority.

The child was aware that these people were his friends and since he wanted nothing more than to please them, his behaviour was exemplary. The school staff proved worthy successors of their founder, Don Bosco - St. John Bosco.

This was a wonderful place, the finest school the boy had attended and his education progressed in leaps and bounds. On Sundays the masters would take their young charges on long excursions, sometimes to Asia Minor, to Scutari and other inland sites. They visited mosques and churches of every denomination and the history of each was outlined for them. Although Bebo had been baptised a Catholic he would not go to confession sticking firmly to his belief in a direct approach to the Almighty. Even this decision was understood and respected by his kindly teachers.

Young Bebo was twelve years old when, for political reasons, the Turkish Government closed the school that had nurtured and protected him.

Italy and Turkey were engaged in the Tripolitanian War. Not only were schools closed but many Italians were deported after Italy annexed Tripolitania, a vilayet of the Ottoman Empire.

Lost without his trusted mentors, Bebo was devastated by the closure and his subsequent move to yet another school. A place had been found for him as a day scholar at the Catholic establishment of Sainte Pulcherie. Resentment oozed from his very being, and trouble was as inevitable as love was elusive. It was just a few months later when a minor incident at the school lit the fuse that once again caused the world of a child to explode around him.

The Brother in charge of the class directed Bebo to stand on a dais in the centre of the room and then he ordered the child to remove his trousers. The instruction was clearly reminiscent of his father's methods of punishment and the boy visibly recoiled. "No!" whispered Bebo. "No!" he shouted. The boy made a move to escape and at the same time the Brother lunged at him. The man's cassock became entangled during the rumpus and the next moment he stood before the class defrocked.

In any other context, the situation would have been hilarious. In shocked disbelief, the master gazed down at his rumpled long underpants before rushing from the room. Bebo stood in stunned silence while the classroom was in uproar as the boys hooted with laughter.

Having heard just one side of the story, the school Director ordered Bebo off the premises and advised him never to return.

There was no alternative but to go and make peace with his aunt and uncle. Arriving at the house, Bebo found only his cousin Angela at home. He sat down and explained the events leading to his expulsion and begged her to help him make her family understand. Things appeared to go well and his uncle wrote to Arthur in an effort to smooth matters over.

A few days later a telegram arrived. 'I am coming to Constantinople,' was the brusque message. Quite obviously, Arthur was not amused.

The following day was Angela's nineteenth birthday and a big party was held for her. Everyone was very busy with the lavish preparations but they still found time to laugh and chatter together. Bebo looked on in envy at the happy household, dreading the moment his father would arrive. Although he was welcome to join the celebrations, Bebo stayed out of the way of the teenage partygoers who were far too sophisticated for him.

The merrymaking seemed to go on forever and Bebo decided to take a look. As he crept along the upstairs landing he heard a muffled scream. Stopping at his cousin's bedroom door he heard her voice pleading with someone to let her go. Quietly he pushed the door open. Angela lay on the bed with her clothes in disarray. A spotty youth had her pinned down with one hand while the other groped her breasts.

Bebo worshipped his cousin and anger welled up inside him as he moved to rescue her. The youth was too big for him to handle alone and so Bebo pulled the heavy key from the door and lunged at the enemy. Unfortunately the attack was overzealous as Bebo misjudged the amount of force necessary. The key cut into the boy's temple and with blood pouring down his face he slumped on the carpet.

The ensuing commotion panicked the frightened child. Racing into the hallway where a panoply of arms decorated the walls, he took a revolver and bullets. Then, for good measure, he grabbed a dagger before running to his room. Locking the door he shouted a warning that he would shoot the first person to enter his room. Hours passed and nothing happened. Peeping from the window he saw the young Lothario leaving under his own steam. Obviously the wound had been nowhere near as bad as he had imagined.

Eventually there came a gentle tap on the door as his cousin tried to tempt him to eat. Angela was in tears, blaming herself for everything that had happened. They both knew that there was no going back and Arthur, when he arrived, would be unyielding.

After Angela had gone he locked the door, wedged a chair under the handle and bolted the window. Pushing the revolver under the pillow he settled down for a sleepless night. It was the early hours of the morning when exhaustion overcame his tormented mind and he fell into a fitful sleep.

Roused by the doorbell, Bebo heard his father's voice echoing around the house. The words 'police' and 'hospital' jumped out of the hubbub going on downstairs.

Time passed and each minute seemed like an eternity as the child awaited his fate. When the knock on his door finally came he held his breath waiting for his father to speak. "Open the door. It's father." Hesitating for only a second, Bebo complied with the order. The gun was removed from his trembling hand and he watched, fascinated, as his father slowly unloaded the weapon.

"Get dressed, you are going away," the boy was told. Two police officers were waiting in the hallway and, as they left the house, Bebo was aware of another policeman who saluted them as they escorted him to a carriage.

The little group travelled to the north of town arriving in the early afternoon at the Chichley Hospital for the Mentally Deranged. The child was ushered into a room and left in the charge of a nun. He was no longer frightened as, thankfully, his father had stayed behind at the house.

A tall, grey haired man quietly entered the room and sat down opposite Bebo. Indicating that the nun could leave, the stranger began to float questions at the boy. "Do you remember your early childhood? Tell me about it! Do you have bad dreams?" All the time the man was smiling, encouraging, giving the boy time to consider both questions and answers. As time went on problems were sandwiched between the questions each with a greater degree of difficulty than the last.

The nun returned to the room, bringing with her light refreshments. The boy heaved a big sigh of relief that his ordeal was over and his mind had been fully investigated. Only when the man returned to probe more deeply into his mental state did Bebo realise they were only half way through the interrogation.

Time dragged and it was evening before the interview was finally over. As he was escorted back to the carriage Bebo began to relax, realising that he had been given a clean bill of mental health. 'That will annoy father,' he thought - giving a mischievous little grin.

Little did he realise how lucky he was. Many people, young

and old, were committed for life to institutions such as the Chichley Hospital, apparently for no reason other than committing a minor misdemeanour.

They drove along the Grande Rue de Pera and the carriage stopped near the three hundred-foot Tower of Galata. Taking the funicular, they arrived at the lower town of Galata, crossed the Galata Bridge and entered Stambul's main police station.

It was the fourth time the child had been in police custody and, as at Aleppo, he was put in a big room full of women. Some were sitting on the floor searching the folds of their garments for lice and, as it was against their religion to kill creatures, they placed them on the floor to seek refuge on another body. Father never wanted me to be in such a place, he told himself.

Wrong! That was exactly what the man had instructed for his youngest son.

The boy stood to the side of the room trying to hide his embarrassment until a girl took pity on him, pulling him down to sit with her. Possibly the girl was a prostitute. Whatever her profession she showed him more kindness than he had seen in a long time. She took charge of him, shared her food and made him a bed at her side.

Pretending he was asleep, Bebo peeped at the rabble surrounding him. Arab women, Turks and Kurds, Armenians and Greeks, - they came from every part of Turkey, from the villages of the Euphrates and Tigris, from Syria and Palestine, from the frontiers of Russia and from Central Asia Minor.

In the corner one group of women seemed to be busy with a form of witchcraft involving a plate of food. They formed horns with their index and little fingers, jabbing at the food. A second group began a funereal song, bowing their heads to the ground and lifting their arms up to heaven. It was a strange chant, beginning mournfully low then gradually rising to shrill peaks.

The inmates had been sitting shoulder to shoulder with little room between them. When one by one they lay on the ground to sleep, their bodies formed a solid mass.

Awaking with a start, Bebo found his nightmare to be reality. As the morning sun streamed through a skylight he began to scratch, feeling the insects crawling inside his shirt. Finding a louse on his chest he killed it in disgust, gaining some satisfaction that his religious scruples did not extend to vermin.

The morning dragged on and his stomach was groaning for food. A guard beckoned him over indicating the door. Trusting he was about to leave the hell-hole, he thanked the girl for her kindness and wished her luck. This was a night he would never forget although it was by no means to be his last experience of prison.

A guard accompanied him back to Galata and the British Embassy. Here he was able to take a bath and rid himself of the smell and the uninvited guests. Feeling relaxed and comfortable in the clothing provided, he was surprised to be led to another cell although the door was left wide open.

It would seem that under the Capitulations a Briton in Turkish police custody had to be handed over to the embassy within a given period of time.

A single visitor called to see him at the embassy, Mr. Edwin Pears, his father's solicitor. "Well my boy, you seem to have upset the whole world. I have arranged for you to go to England. You will sail today. There is no need to worry. In England you will have a new life."

4 Disowned

The sun was already over the yardarm as the Glengoil slipped her moorings and set sail for England. The holds were empty, her cargo of coal off-loaded to help power the industries of Constantinople. Off the port bow, in Asia Minor, the great building of St Joseph's school was clearly visible. Bebo gazed across the channel trying to make out the gardens. What had become of them? What had become of Garcia who had tended the flowers so lovingly? Perhaps his Jewish friend was still in the cells of the Kartal jail.

The white monument erected in memory of his grandfather stood prominently against a backdrop of cypress trees in the Protestant Cemetery at Scutari. A wry smile flickered across the boy's face as he saluted a farewell to his grandfather in the absence of his father.

Further to the right lay Haidar-Pasha and the railway terminal from which the Konia and Tchoumra trains ran. Eyes full of unshed tears, he resisted the magnetic attraction of Constantinople where his father should have been.

The little white house near the lighthouse of Fanaraki came into view. The Princes Islands appeared: Prinkipo, Halki, Oxis and the smaller island - the graveyard of dogs. Between that tiny island and Kartal, far away on the coastline, was the place where Lucy had drowned. He stayed on deck oblivious of the activity around him, alone with his morbid thoughts, until the land disappeared. Then, taking his memories with him, he went below to lie on his bunk.

It was 12th March 1912, two weeks after his thirteenth birthday and Bebo felt no excitement at the prospect of travelling to a homeland he had never seen. Far from it. He would be leaving all he knew and loved, severing precious links - for what? Hostility among strangers, foreigners, in a cold country where they played cricket.

The 8,000 ton vessel progressed through the Sea of Marmara and skirted the Gallipoli peninsula. No-one could have guessed that in just three years the boy would be back at that very place, its tranquillity shattered by war and the sea stained red by the bloody battles of the Dardanelles.

Eventually, with the resilience of a child, he rallied to the sound of voices coming from the galley. Getting to know the members of the crew, he begged them to let him help with the daily chores. Occasionally, he was left alone with the wheel and compass when he would zigzag an erratic course until the steersman came running. Physically fit and with an enquiring mind the boy was kept busy learning a wide variety of new skills.

Payment for his endeavours came in the form of cigarettes and tobacco. By the time they docked in the home port of Middlesborough he had become an inveterate smoker like the rest of his shipmates.

It would seem that his life was to be dogged by policemen. No sooner had they docked at the Yorkshire port than he was informed that a constable was waiting to take him ashore.

This time he was handed over to a priest of the Xaverian Order who escorted him to London and then on to Brighton, where he was to attend the Xaverian College.

From the station, they walked together to Queen's Park. The stately college stood in the grounds. All was sedate, with everything in its place and a place for everything. Tidiness and order were the bywords of this establishment, famous for educating the sons of well-to-do families.

Preferring to keep quiet about his nickname, Bebo discovered that the English version of Adolphe, as he was baptised, was Adolphus. Several weeks passed before he became sufficiently familiar with this new name to react to it when he was spoken to.

Little wonder that Adolphus was a child full of rebellion. Here he was, alone in a strange country and surrounded by boys who acted like lambs. A feeling of isolation almost overwhelmed him; he hadn't a hope of being like his fellow pupils for he just wouldn't know where to start. Come to think of it, he didn't really want to be like them - he much preferred the rabble on the streets of Aleppo.

Starting as he meant to carry on, he lit a cigarette during his first lesson. The action had the desired effect of causing a considerable stir and so he was sent for punishment to Brother Cyril, the head of the school. Hearing that his new pupil had been smoking for some period of time, Brother Cyril struck a bargain with him. The cigarettes and matches would be kept in a drawer in the Head Teacher's office and the boy could help himself at any time. The only condition being that the cigarette must be fully smoked there and then.

Naturally Adolphus felt obliged to test the man's sincerity and later in the day he headed towards the office. Brother Cyril, wearing a benign smile, sat and watched the boy puff away. The next time he knocked at the door the office was empty and so Adolphus helped himself, as arranged, to a cigarette. That was the last time he smoked at the college and he did not understand how astutely the matter had been handled. Brother Cyril had used exactly the same method as Mr. Jenanian in Konia.

Sport played an important part in the school curriculum and Adolphus took an interest in most of the activities, although it was tennis in which he excelled. Even so, he was not distracted from his usual pursuits on the outside. To wander the seafront of Brighton was one of his favourite pastimes.

England in springtime was certainly a sight to behold. Trees and hedges were actively bursting into bud and bulbs of all sorts and sizes were peeping from the recently tended ground. 'There had been nothing like this in Turkey,' he thought. Even the municipal gardens were resplendently decked in a multitude of colour as tulips and daffodils fought for status among the uniform beds. He could almost hear Edwin Pears saying, 'In England you will have a new life.'

It was a nocturnal jaunt into town which was his undoing. Once again he was beset with misfortune when he rounded a corner at midnight to find, as usual, a policeman was on hand to deal with his lame excuses.

The boy was marched smartly back to school and handed over to the head teacher. There was no punishment; Brother Cyril simply informed him that he had outstayed his welcome. The man explained that Adolphus was such a bad influence on the other boys that the only course open to him was to 'insist that Mr. Cooper removes you from this school forthwith.'

No more than three months had passed since his arrival in England and already he was being moved on. The boy was unable to separate the multitude of emotions that invaded his mind. Certainly he resented authority, the lack of understanding and of interest in him - as a person. Equally, he blamed himself. What was wrong with him that everyone disliked him so much? He never wished them any harm. Indeed, he really did want to please them all. Why did he always make such a mess of it?

As one 'new life' ended so the next was about to commence. Forest House School was part of the Monkhams

College, situated at Woodford Green in Essex, only a short distance from London. It was here that the education of young Adolphus Cooper was placed in the hands of one O. P. Masterman Schmitt M.A.

The school had been recommended to the boy's father by the brother of Mr. Agelasto, their neighbour in Tchoumra. There was little doubt, from the attitude of the Principal and staff, that Mr. Agelasto's brother had fully acquainted them with the details of Adolphus' previous misdemeanours - possibly embellished them for good measure. Needless to say the initial introduction left much to be desired and proceeded to go, very quickly, down hill.

A communication was sent to Arthur Cooper in Turkey from the Xaverian College, Brighton. I quote from the original:-

Telegrams: XAVERIANS, BRIGHTON.
Telephone: NAT.1603 KEMP TOWN.

July 17th 1912

Dear Sir,

I thank you for your favour of 9th. Enclosing cheque for £7-4-4, making a total of £30-14-4 received from you. I enclosed a statement showing a credit balance in your favour of 4s-11d, which I am ready to forward to you, should you so wish. I had to send two days ago one of our Masters to Woodford to try to bring your son to his senses, as he was very troublesome. I fear and regret the result is not very satisfactory.

With respectful regards,
I am, dear Sir,
Yours faithfully
J. Cyril Wall

The discipline at Forest House was particularly lax and the boys were allowed out after lessons with little or no supervision. Adolphus had resumed smoking and was now in a situation where it was necessary to raise funds to continue the habit. Enlisting the help of his friend, William, who was also the son of Mr. Masterman Schmitt, the boy set about snaring rabbits in Epping Forest (a talent he had perfected in Turkey).

Armed with wire cord and pegs, the two boys would spend the greater part of their evenings setting traps in the forest. The following morning, before lessons, they would be back to collect their catch which they sold to the school cook.

Rabbits over-ran the forest and before long the enterprising pair had a number of customers, all of whom had been introduced to them by the cook.

The summer holiday was spent with William and his family and for a short while Adolphus settled down. A letter dated 12th September 1912 was sent to Arthur Cooper from Oscar Masterman-Schmitt M.A. in which the head teacher wrote-:

'Now I am happy to state he is just the reverse, one of our nicest boys in the school, as good as gold, obedient and extremely attached to myself... ....You may rest assured that your boy will do well now and that we fully realise the treatment to make your boy an honest, straightforward and steady lad.'

Yes, life was reasonably good. Adolphus had a friend he trusted and, after an initial hiccup, he managed to keep out of trouble. At least for a short period. Close to the school was a private garden in which stood a large greenhouse overflowing with succulent grapes. Adolphus felt his mouth water every time he passed the garden. He loved grapes; they had formed part of his staple diet in Turkey but it was months since he had tasted them. Eventually the temptation was too great for the boy and one quiet evening he climbed the garden fence, pulled himself up on the water butt and attempted to reach the grapes through an open fanlight. For a moment he seemed to hover then the water butt rocked from side to side until eventually it shot from under him cannoning him through the glass with an almighty crash. Somehow his left arm became caught on the wreckage of the roof and blood spurted from his wrist as he hung, suspended from the frame.

Someone came running and an ambulance was called before the boy finally lost consciousness. The stay in hospital was relatively short and upon his return to school, together with the customary letter to his father, his money and cigarettes were confiscated and his friendship with William terminated.

From that moment on he could hardly move within the confines of the school without attracting the enmity of one member of staff or the other. His life was made a misery. He had nowhere to go and no-one to whom he could turn for either help or a little understanding. Certainly there was no point in writing to his father and there was no one else who cared. How he longed for Lucy and how he hated these insensitive foreigners. Matters went from bad to worse until the boy was permanently on the defensive, fighting for his own survival.

Generally unhappy with the reports he was receiving about his son, Arthur again enlisted the help of his neighbour. Mr. Agelasto was in London spending some time with his relations when Arthur persuaded the man to visit Forest House.

The result of this and a subsequent visit was a letter to Arthur written on 7th November 1912, and I quote:-

London 7/XI/12
Thursday

My Dear Cooper,
 I got a few days ago your letter of 22nd and thank you for all your news of Tchoumra and elsewhere.
 On Tuesday I got a wire from Woodford asking me to go there at once and I went yesterday morning.
 M. Schmitt told me that Bebo had been very bad lately.
 Listening to nobody, refusing to do this and that, and when he tried to cane him push his hand in his pocket to get his knive, and began yelling and making a hell of a noise etc etc And he could not keep him any more.
 He wants to send him back to you.
 To this I absolutely objected. I said that it was quite out of the question, that you could not have him back, and that we must consider to put him if possible in a Reformatory or an Institute, we talked the whole position over for about an hour, and called Bebo up and threatened him with the Magistrate, upon which Bebo promised to be good. So Schmitt promised to keep him on for the present. The matter ends there at the moment.
 But I told Schmitt to write and make enquiries at Barnados, at his solicitor etc etc so that when Bebo breaks out again (if he does) to have somewhere to send him.
 I, on the other hand will see if I hear of anything so that I may put him in case Schmitt refuses to keep him.
 I trust that you will approve of any step I may take towards your son and I will do for the best considering
 Bebo does not write to you because he suffers that Mr Schmitt does.
 Give my best regards to M. Laporte and I hope they are getting on well

Remind me to Silovitch and write me a long letter.
Believe me.
  Yours sincerely
  N. J. Agelasto

Bebo, or Adolphus as he was now known, had - on occasions, been digging in his heels and fighting back. He had nothing to lose one way or the other. He was frightened either way, taking punishment or defending himself. Whatever happened, the degree of punishment was the same so he might as well show a little spirit. With just three months to go to his fourteenth birthday he was determined they would not break him.

It never once occurred to him to appeal to his father as after all it was at his father's knee he had his first taste of violence. So yes! He chose to suffer all that Mr Masterman Schmitt did to him for there was no-one else to take his side.

Mr. Agelasto was true to his word and having discussed the matter with his relatives, the Rodocanachi family, who were City Of London bankers, he recommended the New College at Worthing as a possible alternative to Forest House.

Arthur immediately made arrangements to transfer his son and in doing so, avoiding the further shame of yet another expulsion.

A final account from Masterman Schmitt was sent to Arthur in Tchoumra as follows: -

MONKHAMS COLLEGE
AND FOREST HOUSE SCHOOL

Name <u>Adolphus Cooper</u>

                        £   s.   d.

Fees in advance for
.... term. 19
<u>To a/c rendered.</u>   12 :12 : 5

A Subscription of 5/- to cover all extras, such as all Books, Stationery, Games. Ec.....

Dec. 9. 1912

Dear Sir,

      I should be glad if you will let me have a Cheque in settlement of a/c. as there is £4:10:5 outstanding from last a/c., & we cannot allow our a/cs to run on.

      With Kind regards,
      Yrs faithfully
      O.P. Masterman Schmitt. MA
          pp J. Arthur Gates

The bill was receipted on 23/12/12 with a note - balanced by cheque 83544/28058.

The New College, Worthing, was run by a German-Swiss, Mr Baumann. Needless to say the man was fully acquainted with the past of his new pupil, not that it would have made the slightest difference to Adolphus, for he no longer cared. There was a certain inevitability about his school days and now he had the added monotony of living among boys whose greatest crime was to smuggle bullseyes to bed. No longer was he interested in making friends or in pleasing the hier-archy.

As the weeks progressed, Adolphus became adept in the art of self-preservation. He knew exactly when to keep a low profile and somehow managed to avoid any major crisis.

At least, he managed to avoid trouble until the day he fell head over heels in love.

Girls had never figured on his agenda until the fateful day when he glanced up into an incredibly large pair of beautiful dark eyes. Eyes such as he had never expected to see again, eyes so like Lucy's that he held his breath until he was on the verge of losing consciousness. Taking a step backwards, he saw a young girl who was everything that was Lucy.

The vision of Lucy was a pupil at the girl's boarding school situated opposite the New College. That evening found Adolphus wandering in the school grounds on the off chance he would meet with the subject of his reverence again.

Several days had gone by without a single encounter and so Adolphus decided that drastic action was required. As Sunday dawned bright and clear he donned his best uniform, polished his shoes, combed his hair and presented himself for Mass at the local church.

'Lucy reincarnated' was one of several girls who took seats near the front of the sparse congregation. Placing himself in the row behind, Adolphus sat with his eyes glued on the girl while the mass droned on in timeless ritual.

When, at last, the service came to an end the boy waited on the front steps for the girl to join him. "What is your name?" he asked, oblivious of her giggling friends.

"Lucia," she replied.

For a moment the boy was speechless. How far would this coincidence extend? Thinking her questioner was suffering from nerves, the girl continued, "Lucia Valiani, I am from Italy - Palmanova." She explained that she was fifteen years old and very homesick. Her family were hoteliers and had sent her to England primarily to learn the language.

The two youngsters arranged to meet the next evening in the grounds of the girl's school. Lucia was delighted when Adolphus greeted her in her own language and then went on to explain that his own mother was Italian. That was the first of many stolen meetings when they held hands and opened up their hearts. For the first time in years the boy was able to talk about Lucy's death and, for all her youth, Lucia held him gently in her arms as a mother might hold her child.

The Easter vacation arrived in the teeth of a gale. While many children had gone home for the holiday, both Lucia and Adolphus were left in Worthing to their own devices.

Ignoring the storm they made their way along the seafront. The streets and promenade were windswept and empty so they decided to make for the shelter on the leeward side of the pier. Jumping the barriers they held hands and with heads bent low, forced their bodies into the wind as they made for the end of the pier. The planks beneath their feet were shuddering against the strength of the waves and, as they reached some railings, there was a sudden surge of water and Lucia was swept off her feet, slithering and sliding with each ebb and flow of the tide.

"No!" Adolphus was screaming. "No!" He lunged at the girl, grabbing at her dress he hauled her to his side. His arms were round her, holding her so tight she had to fight for breath. Engulfed in a feeling of hopeless terror, the boy shook uncontrollably, remembering how the sea had taken his beloved Lucy. Eventually, soaked to the skin, they headed back towards the promenade but were brought to a halt within seconds as, with a cataclysmic roar, the pier snapped into two.

They clung together for what seemed like hours before rescuers arrived on the scene. "Is anyone there?" a welcomed shout could be heard coming from the beach. With the wind abating and the sea receding, more people began to arrive at the scene. Telling Lucia not to say anything, Adolphus shouted across that they were stranded. A boat was sent for them and once on shore they were wrapped in blankets and taken to the police station.

Glancing around, the boy decided that the establishment had far more to offer than the filthy institutions run by the Turkish police. Accustomed to imprisonment, Adolphus was delighted by their reception at the Worthing Police Station. Plied with tea and biscuits they were given comfortable chairs while they awaited the appearance of their respective head teachers. The boy was still grinning from ear to ear when Mr. Baumann arrived to escort him back to school.

Efforts by both schools to hush up the details of their pupil's involvement and miraculous escape were successful, for the newspapers made no mention of their names. In its report of the events of Saturday, 22nd March 1913, the Worthing Gazette called it a 'memorable storm', and said: 'After the damage had been done, the moon shone out again, and some idea was then given of the magnitude of the disaster. The pavilion, at the sea end, stood there as sturdily as one of the castles of England, the landing stage still resisting the violent buffeting of the tide, whilst the main part of the structure was at the bottom of the sea.'

The children were separated, Lucia being whisked away by an agitated teacher, one Miss Paulette Simmons, who was dressed in a dark grey woollen dress covered by a long, shapeless black cardigan. In the days that followed, try as he would, Adolphus was unable to gain any news of Lucia. The boy had been confined to 'School House', the boarders' residence, and it was almost impossible to make outside contact while matron stood guard. Eventually the fateful day arrived when he was told to prepare to leave.

"Pack your clothes. Your school days are over for good. You are going to sea," said Mr. Baumann prophetically.

5 Embarked

The boy travelled under escort to London's Victoria Station where he was handed over to a jovial young man called Eddie who chatted away incessantly. Several times Adolphus attempted, unsuccessfully, to butt in with a question. As they climbed aboard an open top bus heading towards Paddington the man smiled down at him. "Well," he said, "are you glad you are going to sea?"

So that was it! He was returning to Turkey and the bosom of his family. With mixed feelings he considered the prospect of seeing his father and stepmother again. Before his thoughts could progress along the lines of a possible reunion, his companion explained with enthusiasm. "You are now apprenticed on a ship of the Constantine and Pickering Line. Work hard and you could get on and make something of yourself." So, his childhood was over, left behind with his first love in the south downs of England.

The shipping firm's representative took him by train to Cardiff and from there to Barry Dock. Lying at anchor was the 8,000 ton cargo vessel, Rosewood, one of several owned by the Company all ending in 'wood'. This ship was to be his home for the next few weeks and a trunk full of seaman's clothes, boots and oilskins, sat on the cabin floor awaiting his arrival.

They were to set sail early the next morning and so the young apprentice was advised to get a good night's sleep before embarking on his new career.

Many years were to pass before Adolphus Richard Cooper discovered documents to prove that both his father and his head master had lied to the Shipping Federation about his age. Such was the determination of these two men to rid themselves of the boy.

A letter headed - New College, Worthing, - was sent to Arthur Cooper and read as follows:-

Adolphus has been more trouble to me than any other boy. I had to take him to London and spend a whole day there. I had to wire the Shipping Federation about 6 times in short I would not undertake such a job again.

You know what you paid me and you know what you still owe me; you have my account and the subsequent expenses.

I have done my best for the boy and he has done his worst. I hope he will get on at sea, for on land I am afraid he would not do much good.

Yours faithfully
P. Baumann

On 9th May 1913 a Shipping Federation Consent Paper was completed by Arthur Cooper, who was now employed as an accountant by the Anatolian Railways in Galata, Constantinople. On the form, the boy's date of birth was given as 28th February 1898 instead of the correct year 1899 and his signature had been forged.

A second form headed 'SEA' and 'Form of First Application' was also completed by Arthur who, on behalf of his son, answered 15 years to the question, 'My age last birthday was ....'

In the section above this particular question, it clearly stated:-

The term apprenticeship will be three or four years, and the pay for the period will be about £30 to £40, including rations, with a gratuity of £5 to £10 at the end of the service, payable on good behaviour. Candidates must be between the ages of fifteen and seventeen and a half years, and have the consent of parent or guardian.

They were well under way when Adolphus awoke shortly after dawn. The ship was rolling in a heavy swell as he attempted to climb into the coarse seafaring garb. Swaying from side to side he tried to find his sea legs as he headed for the galley. The Chinese cook grinned at the boy as he offered him a man-sized helping of porridge.

"What's your name?" he was asked as a steaming mug of black coffee was handed across to him. The boy hesitated and was scrutinised by a pair of dark oriental eyes as he searched for an acceptable answer. Were there sailors named Adolphus? he wondered. 'Adolphe' would hardly conjure up the face of a seasoned mariner. Using the shortened form of his middle name, Richard, the boy exclaimed jubilantly. "Dick, Dick Cooper."

The ship's Bosun sent the youngster on to the deck clutching a well-worn hammer. He was to join several seamen who were busy chipping rust from the decks. The language on board was foul with every sentence peppered with four letter words. Dick had no choice but to join the general gab although this was the one vice he had never acquired. With the vocabulary of eight languages on the tip of his tongue he was able to express himself far more colourfully than could be achieved with mere profanities.

The Rosewood was due to unload coal at La Goulette, near Tunis, and load phosphate for Ghent in Belgium. By the time they dropped anchor, Dick had been informed by his shipmates that his meagre annual pay amounted to 'Sweet F.A.' as it simply covered his keep. With his back aching from the hard labour, the boy resolved to jump ship and escape into North Africa.

They were tied up in the six-mile long channel that joined La Goulette with Tunis. Waiting until everyone seemed to be occupied with the unloading, Dick crept ashore unnoticed.

"Salaam Aleikoum (Good morning)," he greeted an Arab on the quayside.

"Aleikoum salaam," the man replied politely.

Dick walked on with a jaunty step, confident that his Arabic would stand him in good stead. Passing through the Porte de France, he made for the Arab quarter where he felt safe. Bedding down for the night in an abandoned old carriage, he realised that hunger pains were clutching his empty stomach. Ignoring his craving for food, Dick slept peacefully until morning.

It was Saturday, the Jewish Sabbath, during which the Jews refrained from making the fires necessary for cooking. Making his way to the Jewish quarter or 'Mellah', Dick set about earning sufficient money for his immediate needs.

Knocking at the door of a low, stone-built bungalow style building, the boy discovered that his fire-lighting services were welcome. Moving from house to house, Dick carried out his new service quickly and efficiently earning one franc for each fire.

Soon he was hurrying back to an Arab eating-house, paying for his meal before taking a seat on the floor. The communal repast of lamb and couscous was set before the diners on a large tray. They ate with their fingers, making little balls of the couscous and flicking it into their mouths. Each time a tasty morsel of sheep was discovered it was kindly offered and, out of politeness, had to be accepted. Thankful for his past experiences with the Arab children, Dick kept a close watch for the most 'delectable' titbit, the sheep's eye! Spotting it at last he plunged in triumph and immediately proffered the eye to the oldest member of the group whom, to the boy's relief, swallowed it gratefully.

Eventually, having eaten his fill and washed it all down with a large cup of black coffee, Dick stepped out into the narrow street. Seconds later there was a shout and as the boy swivelled on his heel, he realised that he was the centre of attention as an Arab policeman gesticulated at him frantically. Obviously he had been rumbled, his disappearance reported. The chase that followed could only be described as a forerunner of a comical silent movie pursuit.

Dick was followed by the policeman and a horde of noisy natives along a twisting and turning labyrinth of alleyways. Leaping on to a low balcony, the youngster lay flat as his pursuers continued onwards waving their arms in child-like excitement. When, after some minutes, the policeman and his entourage had failed to re-appear, the boy decided it was safe to go on. Taking a southerly direction towards the distant hills, he had only gone a few steps when he was spotted by another policeman, this time on a bike. There was little point in resisting as they were now on open ground with nowhere to hide. After token defiance, Dick returned with his captor to the ship where he was locked up until they set sail.

They called briefly at Ghent on their way back to the home port of Cardiff. Here they questioned the young escapee as to the reasons for his disappearance. "I won't work like the rest of them unless I get the same pay," Dick replied. "We'll see about that lad," he was told. The next thing he knew, he was escorted on board the S.S. Hazelwood, outward bound for

Buenos Aires via Las Palmas in the Canaries and Gulfport, Mississippi.

With little choice but to work hard, Dick was learning fast while still resenting his servile existence. Determined to abscond he began to take things more seriously, studying, thinking, planning. With no dock, Las Palmas was out of the question. They anchored offshore and unloaded boxes into flat bottomed barges. The Atlantic crossing to Gulfport was fairly uneventful and Dick showed no interest in going ashore with the rest of the crew when they docked. Although several of his shipmates tried hard to persuade him to join them as his friendliness and quick wit had made him a popular addition to their ranks.

They loaded timber into the massive holds of the Hazelwood and piles of sawn planks were lashed on the decks. Just as the sun began its long climb into the cloudless sky and the ship was almost ready to be cast off, Dick took his chance, scurrying on to the quayside. Hiding behind piles of timber, Dick watched as the ship's hawsers were released and the ship glided away between the islands that protected Gulfport from the winds.

Free at last, the boy decided to stay hidden for a while and hopefully ensure long-term liberty. Eventually, with a nonchalance he didn't feel, Dick left his hiding place and ambled casually into town. Watching and listening very carefully he found great difficulty in understanding the southern drawl of the local inhabitants. By early afternoon he was famished and wondering if it had been quite such a good idea to leave the ship. It was also important to find a suitable place to spend the night before darkness fell.

A luscious display of fruit attracted Dick's attention to a large fruit shop where basket upon basket of succulent grapes made his mouth water. As he drooled on the sidewalk, a plump woman came from the back of the shop tidying the displays and moving gracefully in spite of her size. There was something comforting about the woman who was wearing a black scarf tied behind her head, large earrings and - yes, that was it - a rosary around her neck. Of one thing he was sure, this woman was not American. Seconds later his thoughts were confirmed as a man called to her in Italian saying their daughter was crying.

"Would you give me an apple?" Dick spoke to them in Italian. "I haven't any money."

"*Ma guarda! Ma guarda! Il poveretto. Vienni dentro,*" the woman said, with pity in her voice. The 'poor one' had no hesitation in doing exactly as he was told and he happily entered the house.

It was a delightful household and typically Italian. Several dark headed children moved around the large kitchen helping their mother to prepare a family meal. It was their Neapolitan father, lounging in a large rocking chair, drinking wine, who questioned the newcomer about his movements.

As the unmistakable aroma of spaghetti with a tomato and basil sauce drifted across the room, Dick began to unfold a fictitious story for the benefit of his host. "My name is Francesco Santini." The first name to come readily to his tongue was that of a former schoolmate at the Italian college in Constantinople. "I come from Palermo, I was on a ship and it has sailed without me." Once again the family expressed their sympathy as he sat at the heavily laden table and polished off a huge dish of spaghetti. Although there appeared to be an endless supply of wine, his hosts warned him that as Prohibition operated in the south, alcoholic drinks were officially banned.

Several hours had passed when reluctantly the boy rose from his comfortable seat to take leave of his newly found friends. Waving him back into the chair, the couple sent the children off to play before pursuing a loquacious exchange about Dick's immediate future.

It became obvious to the visitor that while the family wanted him to stay with them, there was just not enough room. The name of the Riverside Hotel was mentioned several times and Dick began to worry about his serious lack of funds. Then he realised they were talking about the possibility of a job for him at the hotel which was run by Greeks.

"I speak Greek," he said quietly, settling the matter.

"I'll drink to that," said Alberto, filling their glasses once again with his own version of 'Grappa', the home made wine of Italian origin. Meanwhile his wife, Maria, rounded up the children and then set off towards the hotel, determined to win over the owner and gain employment for her latest young charge.

The Riverside Hotel was situated opposite the railway station or 'depot' as the Americans called it. The place was always busy, catering for both travellers and townsfolk. Dick stepped into the recently vacated position of dishwasher, answerable to the head cook who was also the brother of the owner. Everything was automated, starting with the delivery of food through a hatch directly to the horseshoe-shaped counter. There were no tables and chairs, just stools at the central counter. Dirty dishes and cutlery rattled along a sloping chute and were deposited at the side of the sink for Dick to deal with post haste. The hours were long and by the time he fell into bed in a room shared with three other lads, his eyes were closed before his head hit the pillow.

Before long it became quite obvious that other activities were carried out in the basement kitchens. Furtive callers to the backdoor were a regular feature of the daily routine. In a matter of days, Dick was involved in the undercover trade of supplying illicit 'booze'. A purpose built inner sanctum housed racks of wines, beers and spirits. There could be little doubt that the two Greek immigrants were making a fortune out of prohibition.

The boy gave serious consideration to staying on at the hotel and eventually gaining American citizenship, but the implant of wanderlust was too strong for him to ignore. A visit to the French Consulate offered a temporary change in fortune.

It was with complete confidence that Dick explained to the French Consul, "I am French. I have been left behind by my ship. Can you help me?"

"Which part of France do you come from?" he was asked.

Oh dear! Although he could speak the language fluently, Dick had never actually been to France. He had heard of Marseilles and of the Canebiere, the main thoroughfare, which the British sailors called the 'Can of Beer'. So Marseilles it had to be.

"Good, I am also from Marseilles," said the consul. "Which street does your family live in?"

"The Canebiere!" Unfortunately no one had bothered to explain that the Canebiere was a street of shops, restaurants and hotels, not dwelling houses.

The consul looked him up and down, shook his head from side to side and eventually said: "Would you like to come here for a while and give my wife a hand? Later we will see what we can find for you."

For a few weeks the pseudo Frenchman became general factotum to the Consul's lady and a companion to her son. Life was easygoing and incredibly boring. Dick was about to plan his next move when the Consul found him a Europe-bound ship.

Expecting a steamship, Dick was surprised and apprehensive to find he would be crossing the Atlantic on an ancient 3000 ton sailing vessel, the Fiora. The old three masted barque was loaded with timber and about to undertake her last voyage to her home port of Genoa.

Officially the cabin boy, Dick was allocated a variety of duties including the supply of stores to the cook, the distribution of daily hard tack rations and, when conditions dictated, a working member of 'all hands on deck'.

The crew was a mixed bag from all corners of the globe, from Puerto Rico, Austria, Finland. The ship's cook, Habanero, hailed from Cuba and in command was one Captain Cattaneo, a Venetian.

They departed Gulfport in April 1914, getting under way at the same time as a Norwegian schooner. For a while, both ships were becalmed, their sails lifeless. A current caught hold of the drifting craft, drawing them together like magnets until there was a clash and rigging pounded on to the decks.

The Fiora anchored up for minor repairs but suddenly a strong wind sprung up and had the ship straining at the leash, transforming her from a lethargic hulk into a streamlined vessel of grace and beauty. They rode the crest of the waves at a merry pace past Key West and into the open seas.

To sail aboard the Fiora was to both love and fear the sea. There were days when the work was almost beyond the endurance of any man and other days when life was pure joy. In calm weather they would fish to supplement their food supplies. Sharks were harpooned and flying fish were caught with a hook and line that tickled the tips of the frolicking waves.

Dick discovered an instinctive passion for sailing and with the agility of a young monkey would scamper around the rigging. There were times when he would climb the mainmast then, sliding down the sloping mainstay, would arrive dishevelled and laughing at the foot of the foremast.

They were sailing waters notorious for the unpredictable changes in weather. The inevitable call for all hands came when a sudden storm blew up, threatening to rip their sails to shreds. Dick raced to the top of the mainmast to help furl the royal. The boy was astride the yardarm when lightening danced along the wire rope he had gripped between his hands. Even as he recoiled from the blow, Dick was catapulted from his perch, falling headlong towards the heaving deck and boiling seas.

As he fell he heard someone screaming. "Lucy! Lucy, help me!" A massive wave hit the deck at the same time he did, cushioning his landing and washing him into a hawser. As the water subsided, he hung on to his lifeline with the last ounce of strength left in his young body. Time and time again the sea tried to drag him from his anchor as he prayed to Lucy. Once again he saw her beautiful face as he prayed for his life. Suddenly he was gripped by strong hands and, barely conscious, he was carried below to safety.

It was some hours before the storm finally blew itself out of existence. The crew was exhausted, with the exception of Habanero who managed to pour a tot of rum for every man and boy. Moving with difficulty across his makeshift bed of sacks to take the proffered cup, Dick realised that his left arm was broken above the elbow. Wincing with the pain, he raised his cup towards heaven giving his guardian angel, Lucy, a grateful salute.

By the time they had set and plastered his arm, Dick was as drunk as a flea in a pint. It was three days before his head stopped pounding and he could return to work, handing out the food and biscuits with his good arm.

There was an Austrian member of the crew, Lorenzo, who came from Trentino although he was far more of an Italian in blood and spirit. Most of the crew had nicknamed him 'Shortie' as he was fairly small in stature but, to make up for his height, he had a wonderfully big voice and on moonlit nights would sit near the capstan playing the mandolin and singing operatic arias. Tough seamen would lounge on the decks listening to the enchanting music with tears in their eyes. In the sea, shoals of dolphins swam alongside as though they too wanted to listen before plunging into the deep.

These were pleasant nights. At other times they were threatened by waterspouts, frightening sights on the horizon that made them hastily change course. Another storm slashed their sails and spares had to be fitted. For weeks they were becalmed and they spent the time repairing the damaged canvas. When the wind came, it was from the wrong direction so they had to tack.

It was the middle of August 1914 when, at last, they neared Gibraltar. They had been at sea for more than four months and the food supplies were almost exhausted. Captain Cattaneo decided to stop the first vessel they met in the busy shipping lanes. They had not been banking on anything as big as the French cruiser that bore down on them just as they hauled up the Italian flag.

As the cruiser 'Bouvet' drew level, her commander hailed the Fiora through a megaphone. "Who are you? What is your load? Where are you bound?"

Captain Cattaneo was puzzled and none too pleased. "Why all the questions?" he shouted back through cupped hands.

"Don't you know there is a war on?" demanded the Frenchman. "Have you any enemy subjects on board?"

The captain and crew of the Fiora looked at each other guiltily. Who was the enemy? In the past months these men had learned to work closely together as a team, essential on a craft such as the Fiora. Suddenly they were made aware that they were not just shipmates but men of many nations.

Captain Cattaneo shouted back that they had no enemy subjects on board and while the rest of the crew bartered for food, their Austrian friend happily sought refuge below deck.

There was a great deal of rejoicing when they sailed into Genoa at the end of their marathon voyage. Apart from anything else the crew had nearly five months pay in their pockets. Certainly a great deal of money for fifteen year old Dick Cooper to manage with any degree of success.

6 Fighting

Leaving the Fiora without a backward glance, the crew fell 'en masse' into the nearest bar. Their youngest member eagerly raised his glass with each toast called for absent friends. Several hours later and still laughing, although he was not always sure what the laughter was about, Dick staggered with his drunken shipmates back to the quayside where they slumped in an untidy heap until morning.

A mere fourteen days of riotous living put paid to his solvent state. Thrusting hands deep into his trouser pockets he discovered that his reservoir of lira had finally run dry. It was well worth it, he thought, trudging down the Piazza Banchi to the docks and, hopefully, another ship.

A few hours later he was climbing on board a Clan Line steamer en route for Algiers. The shipping agent had signed him on as an ordinary seaman, taking the boy's first weeks wage as commission. Seasoned by nearly five months before the mast, Dick undertook his duties with competence and a relaxed humour well beyond his tender years.

Algiers, on the beautiful afternoon of their arrival, presented a shimmering panorama of old white houses closely packed on a hill-side, rising behind modern French buildings that edged the bay.

As he worked on deck, Dick found himself continually glancing towards the town. It was almost as though something was drawing him on to dry land. That evening he left the ship and walked to the Place du Guvernment at the foot of the old town. Attracted by the sounds of merrymaking, he continued along the Rue de la Lyre turning into a cafe from which echoed the sounds of lively music and boisterous laughter. Young people and soldiers of the Zouave Regiment were singing and dancing while an older man squeezed joyful sounds from a battered old accordion.

Sitting to the edge of the cheerful group, Dick ordered coffee. As the cup was placed on his table by a smiling Arab waiter, a youth reached across and promptly poured the contents of his cup into a flowerpot. Dick was up, kicking his chair out of the way as he prepared to fight the stranger. Then, to his surprise, he realised there was no anger or malice in the young man's face, in fact he was grinning at Dick for all he was worth. "You don't want coffee," he said. "Waiter, bring wine!"

They had finished their first bottle of cheap red wine and Dick had ordered a second before introductions were formally carried out. It seemed his bronzed companion was a Parisian by the name of Marcel Mozzi. Others drifted over to join them and the conversation turned to war. "I am joining the Foreign Legion in the morning," boasted Mozzi. Several others agreed that they too were headed for the Legion Headquarters.

By this time Dick's thoughts were slightly muddled by the wine. "What is the Foreign Legion?" he demanded loudly.

Mozzi was only too willing to explain. "It is a regiment that anyone can join. They don't ask for papers, they don't want to know your age or your background. They take anyone who is fit and healthy."

Here was a call to action! Dick would follow the brave Mozzi and his companions. They would fight side by side for freedom. Good against evil. By this time they could hardly stand let alone fight. In ones and twos they wobbled out of the cafe, teetering on the brink of consciousness. Behind them came Mozzi and Cooper, brothers at arms - or rather, brothers in each other's arms for they certainly could not stand alone.

It was early morning before they finally lurched towards the recruiting office in the Rue de la Marine. Having reached their goal they abandoned themselves to oblivion beneath a nearby archway.

A few hours later, Dick and his new found friend Mozzi tried their best to smarten their dishevelled appearance before joining a disorderly queue of would be Legionnaires.

"What do *you* want?" snapped an orderly when Dick arrived at the desk.

"To join the Legion."

"Have you brought your nursemaid with you?"

The man's sarcasm on top of Dick's thumping headache riled the boy, but he managed to keep his temper. "I am twenty-one," he stated firmly.

The orderly left the desk and crossed the room to speak to an officer. Both men eyed the boy as they whispered together for a minute. Finally they both came over and looking directly into Dick's eyes the officer snapped: "If the doctors pass him as fit, take him!"

The doctors gave him a clean bill of health and he moved on to a room where Mozzi was already signing papers. A questionnaire was thrust into his hands.

Name: *Jean Cornelis Debruin.*

He wrote the first name to come into his head, that of a Dutch sailor from his last ship.

Nationality: *Mexican.*
Place of Birth: *Vera Cruz.*
Age: *21.*
Date of Birth: *1893.*

His befuddled mind had to struggle for several minutes before he managed to give the correct year of birth to suit his sudden coming of age.

The details on the completed form, headed: 'Enlistment in the French Foreign Legion for the duration of the war', were read back to him before he was asked to sign. The date was 8th October 1914. Dick Cooper - now to be known as Jean Cornelis Debruin - was fifteen years and seven months old, a Legionnaire de 2me Classe and the youngest Legionnaire in the history of the French Foreign Legion.

Many years later, looking back on this day, Dick Cooper was to make the following comments:-

'To sum up the Foreign Legion, one has to explain the psychology of the Legionnaire. Few writers have achieved success in their attempts to throw light on this passionate subject. Attempted explanations are complicated by the fact that the Legion is composed of men of many races, whose origins, sentiments and ideas are totally different. This in itself gives the Legionnaire an indefinable personality of his own.

The Legion is a refuge, a meal ticket, a place for rehabilitation. It can also be a profession. A man goes to it without identity papers, with the nationality of his choice, and free of all criminal records. He leaves his past outside the recruiting-office door. In the Legion one finds strange mixtures of good and bad, latent heroism, and sometimes a degraded soul. All these aspects, when fused together, emit an iron energy, an instinctive zest for adventure, an astonishing fount of initiative and a supreme disdain of death. This composite Legionnaire has all the sublime virtues brought out by war and displays virility and superiority. Yet he lives in a fantasy world, and if ever he is in trouble he will blame *le cafard*, a name adopted by Legionnaires to mean a form of temporary madness peculiar to the Legion, brought about by a variety of circumstances, including boredom. But, above all, the men of the Legion religiously uphold their traditions and military integrity.'

On the day of their enlistment, Cooper and Mozzi were sent to the Caserne Vienot, at Sidi-Bel-Abbes, at that time the Headquarters of the Legion. No sooner had they arrived than there was news of an Arab revolt in the Algerian interior.

Without so much as initial training, they were handed uniforms and rifles and then, unceremoniously, dumped on a train heading towards the troubled area. It was en route that they learned to load their rifles, a Mark Gras, the type used in the Franco-Prussian War of 1870. When Dick attempted his first shot, from an upright position, he was knocked sprawling. Getting to his feet, he made matters worse by trying to unload the spent cartridge with a pencil. The 'old sweats' had many a laugh at the boy's antics but, nevertheless, they taught him all he needed to know, including the sharp pull on the rifle bolt needed to eject the cartridge case.

The battalion managed to quell the insurgent tribesmen and then continued on to Tiaret, where the new recruits were given some formal training to add to that already received in the field. During the spring of 1915, Dick Cooper and Marcel Mozzi joined the newly formed 1st Regiment de Marche d'Afrique, under the command of Commandant Geay. This was to be a follow up force after the Gallipoli landings of the British and Anzac troops in their ill-fated attempt to smash through Europe's back door. The history books have since been filled with accounts of the initial Gallipoli landings. Few go on to acknowledge the very real presence in that hell-hole of the men of the French Foreign Legion in April 1915.

The account kept by a young man who had celebrated his sixteenth birthday only thirty-six days earlier must be considered invaluable.

In a diary he kept for his father Dick Cooper wrote:-

5th April   *Embarked on the Carthage at Oran. All the battalion feels happy. Played cards with Marcel Mozzi, Piccini and Dixon. Don't know our destination.*

8th April   *At Valetta, Malta. Heard of the sinking of the Bouvet. Apparently sunk inside the Dardanelles on 18th March. She was the cruiser who helped us with food on the Fiora*

11th April   *At Alexandria, in Egypt, we disembarked today and are camping near the Victoria Hospital, Sidi-Bish. General d'Amade, is the Commander-in Chief of the French Forces, he passed us in review. He was with General Ian Hamilton, the British Commander.*

22nd April   *We are in the Bay of Mudros on the Island of Lemnos. Ships everywhere, British and French, hundreds of them.*

25th April   *The British are making the initial landings on the peninsula. The River Clyde has been driven on shore and the British are using it as a landing stage.*

The 25th became known later as Anzac day. At the time of writing the diary, no-one knew of the blood-bath going on along the Gallipoli coast.

26th April   *French 175th Regiment of Infantry landed reinforcements.*

The French Foreign Legion battalion landed on V beach. They had left Mudros harbour on the morning of 28th April for Sedd-el-Bahr. On the Asiatic side the guns of Kum-Kale and Chanak fired without mercy as the Legionnaires also used the stricken River Clyde to their advantage, clambering across it to a deserted beach.

All around them was mute evidence of the holocaust that had gone before. The sea was full of bodies, held beneath the shallow water by the weight of their packs. Despite their terrible losses, the British had pushed the Turks back.

As they passed through the village of Sedd-el-Bahr, with its fortress on their right hand side, Dick stopped to gaze at the bodies of two Turkish soldiers. What was he doing here? What were any of them doing here? These people were his friends! As he stared at the two men, lifeless, twisted in their passing, war took on a whole new meaning.

The men were told to rest for a while. Rain was pouring through the branches of the olive trees and they used their ground sheets as capes. Snipers were taking pot-shots in the pitch black of the night and the occasional bullet whistled past. A voice shouted at them, "Come here, you, you and you!" Adjutant Chef Leon appeared next to them and indicated that Dick and two of his companions, Parentie and Keller, were to scout for the Tenth Company. "They must have strayed," he said.

Dick was sent to the right. Behind him was Morto Bay. Ahead could be anyone or anything and the boy was scared stiff as he melted into the darkness. Aware only that he was climbing uphill, Dick suddenly heard voices. His rifle was ready loaded and his hands tightened on the weapon as he stood motionless. Just ahead he could make out shadowy figures and a Turkish voice called: "Kim dir (Who is it)?"

Oh hell! He was behind enemy lines. Now what? "Ben,

Ben, Achmed," he called, using a name as common in Turkey as Smith in England.

Keeping well below the skyline, the boy could see a number of Turks outlined higher up the hill. Gaining confidence, he called out a warning that there were French soldiers close by. Unfortunately it had the wrong effect; they hurried towards him rather than in the opposite direction as he had planned. He thought about running but realised he would have no chance of dodging the bullets that would surely follow. The idea that came to him was prompted by a genuine need. The boy immediately dropped his trousers and crouched down on his haunches. Seeing nothing but a shadowy outline behind a bush, the men veered off, calling him to get a move on.

The minute the Turks were out of sight, Dick ran as though all the demons of the night were hot on his heels. Again and again he lost his way until he finally saw the sea ahead. 'Morto Bay' he whispered to the night, or was it somewhere entirely different? He had to admit that he had no idea where he was.

Figures appeared just ahead and he shouted "*Burda guelme*! (Don't come here)." Bullets clipped the rocky ground as he dived for cover. Oops, wrong country, he decided. The only trouble was, from which country were they? The decision had to be quick and, please God, the right one. "La Legion, La Legion," he yelled at them, crouching low and ready to run should the firing start again. Thankfully, this time he had made the right choice and was welcomed back by men of his own Company.

For two days the battalion waited for orders. They were camped close to the fort of Eski-Hissarlik above Morto Bay. Far below them was the Queen Elizabeth, the British Flagship, with Admiral de Robeck and Commodore Keyes on board. From the Elizabeth they were shelling Achi-Baba, the big hill behind the village of Krithia, and periodically turning her mighty guns on Kum-Kale, the fort on the Asiatic coast.

The hours dragged by and there was plenty of time for reflection as they awaited the inevitable, knowing this was the lull before the storm. On the morning of 1st May all hell was let loose. Dick lived through the next few hours in a complete haze. Certainly he carried out orders as fast as they came, vaguely aware that in doing so he stood the best chance of survival. The Turkish troops charged with fixed bayonets and at the same time their 75-mm guns pounded incessantly. It seemed impossible that anyone, of either side, could live through such an abiding hell.

The fighting continued on the 2nd and 3rd May until the men of the Foreign Legion found themselves above the Kereves Dere ravine, nicknamed the Ravine of Death. Once again they waited, taking shelter wherever possible. Dick lit a cigarette and Legionnaire Elvin, who was facing him across a hollow, rose to get a light. As Dick held his cigarette out towards the man a shot rang out and Elvin fell. The bullet had entered the back of the man's head and came out in the centre of his forehead. As the boy looked on in horror Elvin sat up as if pulled by a spring, opened his eyes and stared blankly before crumpling into the mud.

As the men sat in silence staring down at Elvin, they were transfixed. Then the order came that they were to storm the Kereves Dere. They stood in a single line ready to leap, one at a time, into the ravine. The first man jumped - and died, a bullet through his head. The second, third and fourth all suffered the same fate as the Turkish marksmen proved their worth. Dick was fifth in line. Swerving as he went, the boy dived headfirst over the top griping his rifle with both hands and rolling over as he hit the ground. A bullet had clipped his heel but he was safe, up, running for shelter, and yelling upwards: "Keep changing! Some dive, some jump." Gaining the comparative safety of an overhang the boy started rapid covering fire and was soon joined by the others, all of whom made the descent without further casualty.

For his initiative and bravery young Dick Cooper (in the name of Jean Cornelis Debruin) was awarded the Croix de Guerre. It was the first Croix de Guerre to be won by the Foreign Legion and believed to be the first such award in all the French Forces, just as Dick was believed to be the youngest combatant in those forces. (The details were later transferred to Dick's real name.) The medal had been instituted less than a month earlier on 8th April 1915. His citation read 'Tres belle conduite au feu'. Perhaps it was due to Dick Cooper's nationality, an Englishman, that so little has previously been recorded about this notable event.

Losses were heavy. The Legion had lost six hundred of the one thousand in the initial landings. During the nights of 9th and 10th May the Turks attempted to regain some of the lost ground but were successfully repelled.

Dick had been detailed as a runner and was making regular journeys to and from 'V' Beach. The 11th May found him once again heading for the beach, this time to load food on to mules. As he reached the castle of Sedd-el-Bahr he saw a group of Turkish prisoners under British guard. Unnoticed by the guards he sat among the fifty or so Turks talking to them, mainly about places he knew. One man, from Konia, was intrigued to find a French soldier who knew so much about his home town. When Dick tired of the conversation and realised he might be missed, he rose to leave and join his comrades.

"Sit down there," he was told by a British soldier. Hell, I've done it now, he thought. How do I get out of this one? His clothes had long since lost any resemblance to a uniform and his buttons, with the Legion Etrangere motif, had been swapped for tins of British jam and bully beef. He tried to explain who he was but seemed to be getting nowhere until a British news reporter, Ellis Ashmead-Bartlett of the Daily Telegraph and official war correspondent at the Dardanelles, approached them.

Ashmead-Bartlett listened to what the boy had to say and then called over a French officer who, for good measure, summoned Legionnaires from the beach to identify him.

The following day a group of Legionnaires, including Dick, were detailed to dig the graves of fallen comrades in an area close to Morto Bay. They were working late into the night when a series of ear-shattering explosions made them dive for cover. Realising the commotion was out at sea, the men stood peering across the bay which, by now, was clearly visible from the light of a burning ship. The British cruiser Goliath had been crippled by a Turkish destroyer and was sinking fast. Terrible screams could be heard from the men going down with their ship, just six hundred yards from Sedd-el-Bahr.

The Legionnaires stood in absolute silence. One or two, with eyes closed, moved their lips in silent prayer. The boy who stood with them shivered. The cold began to creep slowly along every inch of his spine until he was frozen to the spot. The French soldiers remained motionless, surrounded by the open graves, until the light was finally extinguished as the ship slid into her watery grave and there was an unforgettable sound of silence.

Two days later, Dick stood alone in the night with the stench of the dead searing his senses. He wanted to go home, to leave the obscenity that was war. Gazing into the night he thought of his father. The beatings he had received at the hands of that man were forgotten, paled into insignificance by recent events.

Father would be so proud of me, he thought. Closing his eyes he could see the smile upon his father's face as he read the citation, *Tres Belle Conduite au Feu*. Yes! He was going home. He gave no conscious thought to the fact that he would be deserting in the face of the enemy, and would be guilty of cowardice. All he wanted was to get away, for which the penalty was death.

Two or three miles across the Dardanelles lay Asia and that was his destination. Stripping, he tied his clothes in a bundle on to his back and eased himself into the water. Thoughts of a happy reunion disintegrated as he was gripped in a rapid current flowing from the Sea of Marmara to the Aegean. It seemed he would go, incongruously, the way of Leander, the Romeo of the Dardanelles, who drowned in the strait while making his nightly swim to visit Hero, his Juliet.

No matter how hard he fought the current, he made no headway. All thoughts of his family had drowned in the treacherous seas. Lucy; he could see her as he drifted with the current towards Sedd-el-Bahr. It was Lucy who gave him the strength for one last supreme effort to clear the current. Naked, he landed below the old castle close to V Beach, a good eight miles from his Company at Kereves Dere.

The task of pulling on his sodden clothing sapped what little strength he had left. Sinking down to squat on his heels Dick realised that he was shivering uncontrollably. He had to get moving, apart from which he had to rejoin his company before daylight. The journey was a nightmare, the direction - a matter of guesswork and plain good luck. At times he crossed makeshift graveyards where the corpses were barely covered. The sun was just rising as he found his company. It was obvious that he had not been missed and luckily there had been no attack during the night to reveal his absence.

The fighting continued for days on end. The battles were of the bloodiest; the losses on both sides, catastrophic. It was a hell on earth that brought out the best in some and the worst possible evil in others. The boy endured days of sheer horror with the resilience of a child, seeing only what he wanted to see, leaving questions unasked. He lived in hope, forcing himself to be worthy of his uniform, even though it hung from his lean body in tatters, unrecognisable even to himself.

On more than one occasion he found himself in British

lines. It wasn't his army and so he would brazenly approach the officers, the higher the rank the better. One morning he ran into the famous General Hamilton who was strolling with General Braithwaite. "Good morning. How is the war on your side?"

"Who the hell are you?" General Hamilton asked.

"A Foreign Legionnaire and I am British," Dick answered proudly.

"Good God, you are only a boy," came the surprised reply.

"Not any more, sir. I am a man with the Croix de Guerre."

The Generals raised their eyes, smiled at each other and continued on their way oblivious that the child was telling the truth and genuinely held the French medal.

For several days both sides had been attacking and counter-attacking to gain and regain a stretch of land known, because of its shape, as the Haricot. On the 22nd May it was the turn of the Turks to make the assault and the fighting was particularly heavy. Dick was in a trench when suddenly the men to either side of him were shot and as the Turks overran their position, bayoneted. In the skirmish the boy lost his rifle and dropped to his knees. With eyes on the enemy he felt for the missing weapon but, instead, he found a hand grenade. 'I will take them with me,' he determined, pulling the pin and dropping the grenade. Looking up, he realised that the Turks had over-run their position and, with the exception of bodies, he was alone. With just seconds between life and death, Dick threw himself into a trench at right angles to the one about to explode.

Shells seemed to be bursting all around him, as though both sides were throwing everything they had directly at him. He lay hugging the ground at the bottom of the trench until he became aware of the confused sound of a counter attack. Turks pounded over him with Legionnaires hot on their heels. Retrieving his rifle, Dick joined the fray.

The diary continued:-

23rd May   *Italy has declared war against Austria.*

25th May   *Heard that a British cruiser has been sunk opposite Gapa-tepe by the German submarine U21. 71 men lost.*

27th May   *British warship Majestic torpedoed by U21 sunk off Sedd-el-Bahr.*

29th May   *Visit to the Askold.*

The Askold was a Russian cruiser known as the 'Packet of Woodbines' because of her five-funnels. After a month of fighting the Legionnaires were to be taken to the island of Tenedos by the Askold. No sooner had they been welcomed aboard the vessel than the guns of the Turkish artillery batteries, hidden on the coast of Asia Minor, began a heavy barrage. Russian sailors manned the ship's guns watched closely by the Legionnaires. A man turned a wheel and a large shell came up; a second man slammed the shell into the breech, and a third pulled an attachment of wire to fire the weapon. The Askold took a direct hit, killing all three members of the gun crew. For a moment the Legionnaires stood looking at the scene in horror, then, Piccini moved forward and started to turn the wheel. Mozzi began the loading, leaving the firing to Dick. They successfully dispatched three shells before the agitated activities of the Russians alerted them to a problem. The ship had turned and the three volunteers had been hurling shells close to the Allied GHQ, Gallipoli.

On 4th June they were still fighting in the area of the 'Haricot'. Lieutenant Leon led the last twenty of the original landing party into battle with bayonets fixed. At the end of the day many thousands were dead, Lieutenant Leon seriously wounded and of the 'twenty' only seven survived.

6th June   *Turkish 9th storm our lines.*

7th June   *Bad weather - strong winds.*

17th June   *At last the weather breaks.*

On 21st June a general attack on the 'Haricot' included the Seven Originals. At 3.30pm they were ordered to charge the Turkish trenches and, as he ran, Dick saw Mozzi fall in front of him. As the boy ran on, he could see barbed wire ahead. From the left a Turkish machine-gun was sweeping the ragged waves of men as they surged forward. Unpinning a hand grenade, Dick threw it in the direction of the gun which ceased firing. The action had distracted his attention from the barbed wire and so, before he realised the danger, he was caught in the wire and a sitting target for Turkish marksmen.

Struggling desperately, Dick managed to free himself from the wire. His hand was dripping with blood and he realised that it was shrapnel that had caused the injury, not the barbed wire. The hand was useless, gashed wide open reminding him of the grape-stealing injury of earlier days. As he ran to his own front line trenches he was grabbed by a 'Medic', "That's the end of the Dardanelles for you!"

Dick made his way to the beach where a doctor checked his wound and gave him a label marked, 'For Evacuation'. As he waited at the casualty clearing station, Dick saw Legionnaire Parentie with a bullet hole through his left shoulder. "Shake," said Parentie. "You and I are the last of the thousand. The other five died today."

The boy staggered forward and dropping to his knees he said a silent prayer for his friend Mozzi. For a moment he was back in the café in Rue de la Lyre with Mozzi laughing at him and offering him his friendship.

7 Guest

The evacuation of the wounded was disorganised and deeply traumatic to both the participant and the observer. A mixture of stretcher cases and walking wounded were directed to vie for places on a tiny jetty. A small boat was used to transport these evacuees out to the Canada, a former luxury liner recently converted into a Red Cross ship.

There was little luxury to be found now on-board the overcrowded Canada. The nurses worked flat out in a super-human effort to make amends for the serious shortage of doctors. In turn, the walking wounded assumed the role of nurse or orderly in issuing and emptying bottles or bedpans, administering water and comforting the dying.

The sixteen-year-old worked along side his comrades, glad of the distraction that gave him little time to think about the horrendous injuries and the screams of those suffering unrelenting pain.

Eventually they docked at Sidi Abdullah, Tunisia, southwest of Bizerta. The hospital there was already full to overflowing and the latest arrivals were placed in makeshift cots, outside, under decorative arches. This proved to be a distinct advantage as the heat inside the hospital building was overpowering.

Once again the boy was helping wherever and whenever possible but a week had passed without his own wound being dressed. The doctor did not seem unduly concerned as Dick was undoubtedly strong and healthy. Once a clean dressing was applied to his injury, Dick was offered a three-week pass with instructions to report to the Fort St. Jean, Marseilles, at the end of his leave.

Paris! The first place to spring to mind and one that required no further consideration. Paris here I come, thought this strange mixture of man and boy identified by his assumed name of Jean Cornelis Debruin.

The journey took him by way of Marseilles where the majority of his pay disappeared over the counter of a dubious looking cafe. Somehow he made it to the Gare de Lyon in Paris by which time both his stomach and his pockets were empty.

The railway station had a first aid post where Dick had his wound dressed. The bustling nurse on duty was busy directing soldiers to a free buffet, run by members of the Dame de France group, placed on the far side of the station. The boy needed no second biding and was hungrily tucking into a huge bowl of soup when a familiar figure made his way towards him.

Legionnaire Maresca, a Spaniard born in Algeria, was one of the biggest villains in the Legion. He had long ago perfected the art of Systeme Debrouillage, known as System Demerde or System D - a method of using your wits to acquire whatever you wanted by fair means or foul. Maresca was a man without conscience, an accomplished scrounger, sometimes worse. At this moment, to Dick, he was also a friendly face.

The boy was persuaded to return to Marseilles and so the two Legionnaires boarded the overnight train for the southern port. Once again the pair became guests of the Dame de France, this time for a welcome breakfast. Swallowing the last dregs of coffee, Dick was pulled from his chair by an enthusiastic Maresca who announced that they were about to attend Mass at the church on the Quai des Belges.

Amazed by the latest decision of his doubtful travelling companion, Dick suddenly realised that church was the sanctuary he needed. Church was the one place he could talk to someone who would listen, someone who would not expect too much of him, someone who would understand and might even help him to understand. He desperately needed to understand all those sights and the sounds he could never put into words, the futility of war, the degradation of human minds and bodies. Just as a lamb is led to the slaughter, so Maresca guided Dick into the hushed precincts of the beautiful waterside church.

Throughout the service the boy's thoughts were no more than a jumbled mess, flashbacks of people and places; his father, Lucy, Farez and Garcia, Kartal, Konia, Woodford and Worthing. As he closed his own eyes he could see others reflected, peering at him from the waters surrounding V Beach. He recognised an image of Legionnaire Elvin staring unseeingly across no-man's-land to the distant horizon. Quickly he opened his eyes and gazed for several minutes at the roof of the magnificent building. The next time he bowed his head in prayer the haunting eyes became huge black grapes floating on the incoming tide, washed up on a Sussex shore at the feet of his outraged stepmother. Several times he experienced waves of giddiness that left him feeling physically sick.

Rising from his knees, Dick sat back on the carved wooden bench and gazed at the head of his friend. Maresca was mumbling a meaningless gabble while clutching a rosary to his heaving breast. Ignoring the exaggerated theatrics at his side, the boy glanced around the otherwise peaceful retreat. Catching the eye of a well dressed and happily smiling lady,

Dick quickly lowered his eyes in embarrassment. Glancing back up, he saw the smile had deepened and that the wearer was approaching from the side aisle. From a distance she had appeared to be young but now, as she drew near, he would judge her to be middle aged, fiftyish. Even to his inexperienced eye it was obvious that this was a woman of breeding and substance.

Maresca chose this moment to hurriedly complete his counterfeit devotions, greeting the lady like a long lost friend. "Madame, it is so delightful to meet with you. We have just returned from fighting in the Dardanelles. It is too long since we have attended Mass." With hardly time to draw breath Maresca continued. "We are on leave but we have no family to visit."

Dick began to understand the charade. This was System D at work. Maresca had known that this woman would be here. He had been waiting for her.

"You poor boys, you must come to lunch with us." The lady handed over a visiting card and peering over the shoulder of his companion, Dick saw the word 'Countess'. Yes! There could be no doubt that Maresca knew exactly what he was doing. The youngster was painfully aware that he had been cleverly used by his friend to attract the attention of the kindly woman.

As they entered the home of the Countess near the Porte d'Aix, on the other side of the Cour Belsance, Dick was reminded of the luxurious hotel of Monsieur Soulier in Konia. The guests were shown into a magnificent salon where Persian carpets littered an otherwise shining floor. Elegant tables strained under the weight of silver and crystal and the walls were steeped in gilded mirrors.

It was only by chance that Dick saw Maresca's sleight of hand as the man skilfully removed a silver box from a side table. "Put it back!" Dick spat out quietly at his companion.

Raising his eyebrows and with a nonchalant shrug of his shoulders, Maresca held the box up towards the heavily draped window before depositing it carefully back on the table.

The Spaniard proceeded to make matters worse as he wolfed down his food, pocketing the cutlery at the end of each course. The man appeared to be without feeling as Dick steadily kicked his shins in a desperate effort to restrain his unscrupulous instincts.

Eventually the nightmare was over as Maresca decided to take his leave plus a few other knick-knacks for good measure.

For a while Dick sat quietly, mortified by the behaviour of a fellow Legionnaire. Eventually he said, "I am so sorry. I am afraid some things have been stolen from you."

The Countess smiled, "I know. I saw it all. If it will help, then so be it."

Later that day the Countess introduced Dick to her lovely, elegant, and most definitely emancipated, niece. The young woman, in her twenties, was dark and shapely. The boy, so recently from the battlefield, took one long look at her sparkling eyes and was spellbound.

"'Allo Militaire" she greeted him, planting a kiss firmly upon his open mouth.

That evening they left the Countess in her sumptuous surroundings and they wandered hand in hand through the Place d'Aix to the girl's apartment. The days that followed were idyllic. Dick was mere putty in the hands of the beautiful Stephanie. She was demanding both in love and in life, always wanting her own way and always getting it as she fashioned a fairy tale route away from reality.

Inevitably their days were filled with sunshine as they strolled hand in hand on the headland, gazing out across a shimmering sea to where the Isle D'If majestically guarded secrets of old. Evenings were spent in the quayside cafes sampling the local brew and exchanging stories from the past.

They were in no hurry to leave the lovely old port and return to the apartment, certain they would eventually welcome the new day in each other's arms.

The wound that had so fortuitously given him leave was now healed and it was time to report to the Fort St Jean for orders. Dick had reckoned without the determination and ingenuity of his paramour.

Stephanie had decided upon a fake accident whereby it would appear that Dick had fallen from a tram. An ambulance would be called and evidence established that Dick was not fit to return to his regiment.

The events duly took place and the ambulance transported him to the Hopital Militare. Stephanie explained to everyone who was prepared to listen that the boy had been suffering from giddy spells - this indeed was not far from the truth although Dick persistently refused to acknowledge the fact. Finally a doctor diagnosed a 'comotion cerebral' (cerebral irritation) having caused a hysterical fit and this earned the reluctant soldier several more weeks in the arms of his lover.

Inevitably the rude awakening arrived in the form of an armed guard who swiftly escorted Dick to the Fort St Jean and a waiting ship headed for the Dardanelles.

The return voyage to Gallipoli was broken by an overnight stop on the Island of Mudros. Pining for the beautiful Stephanie and determined to drown his sorrows, Dick managed to barter successfully with the local Greeks for Samos wine. Getting together with a number of his comrades, spare boots were exchanged for two goatskins of the heady wine.

Five of them sitting around a table shared the skins, taking turns to squeeze a jet of wine into their mouths. They bandied yarns as they gargled and swallowed the sweet wine made from figs and tasting like syrup. Suddenly one of the group stood sharply to attention muttering something about needing more wine. He left the room with the suddenness of someone who has remembered an important errand. One by one the others followed suit.

Left alone at the table, Dick tried to make sense of his comrade's disappearance. Alarm bells were ringing somewhere at the back of his drunken mind. Rising unsteadily to his feet the boy equipped himself with a sturdy lump of wood to fight off the attack he believed was waiting on the other side of the rickety door.

The next morning a heaving, grumbling heap of five Legionnaires awoke with bleary eyes and splitting heads to find the only treachery had been tapped from within the goatskins.

Dick's return to the Gallipoli peninsula must rank as one of the shortest. He was landed at V Beach during a bombardment and after taking just two or three steps was hit by a large piece of shrapnel which painfully penetrated his right thigh. It seemed a lifetime since a bullet had entered almost the same spot when he had been running with the Young Turks in Constantinople. Thinking back, a lot had happened in those seven intervening years.

Minutes later he was rushed on-board the Canada as she was again preparing to leave with her decks full of injured veterans.

By now the bed shortage in Bizerta was acute and so the Canada was re-routed to Bone where the injured men were dispersed to several centres. Dick was taken to the Vaccaro Hospital which had been converted from a school and it was there he met a wonderful family, the Mairs, who hailed from bonny Scotland.

Mr Mair, who was a representative of a British coal firm in Bone, Algeria, was a frequent visitor to the Vaccaro Hospital giving help where he could but in particular to British soldiers. It was inevitable that the man and his family took young Dick Cooper firmly under their wing. The boy spent many happy weekends at the Mair's elegant villa beside the sea at St. Cloud, on the outskirts of Bone. For a while Dick had a family such as he had never known, for these were people with hearts of pure gold.

Eventually and inevitably his carefree lifestyle had to end. His presence had been drawn to the attention of one Herbert Scratchly, the British Vice-Consul. Mr Scratchly insisted that the boy move into the Consulate where he was constantly quizzed about his past. Before very long, plans were afoot to obtain Dick's discharge from the French Foreign Legion.

The discharge procedure was bound to be long and complicated as the boy had lost touch with his family and was also serving as a Legionnaire under an assumed name.

On the declaration of war, Arthur Cooper had chosen to take his family to Italy rather than be interned in Turkey. Mr. Scratchly was not to be deterred and with sheer persistence he traced Arthur by contacting The Shipping Federation who, in turn, obtained Arthur's address by way of the Gresham Life Assurance Society.

A letter from the Shipping Federation, St. Mary Axe, London, dated 12th October 1915 was sent to Arthur Cooper Esq., at 11, Via Solferino, Milan. It read:-

Dear Sir,

We have received information from Herbert Scratchly Esq., The British Vice-Consulate, at Bona, Algeria, on the question of identifying a lad who states he is your son, Adolphus Richard, apprenticed in 1913 to Messrs. Constantine Pickering & Co., and shipped on their S/S "Rosewood". You will remember that he deserted the company afterwards and appears to have joined the French Foreign Legion. After having been wounded in the Dardanelles, he now appears to be anxious to be claimed by you. Will you be good enough to communicate with the British Vice-Consulate at Bona? Your address was furnished by the Gresham Life Assurance Society, London.

> *Yours faithfully,*
> *Michael Brett,   Secretary.*

In the meantime Herbert Scratchly had also written to Constantine and Pickering. Their reply dated Friday 22nd October 1915 read:-

Dear Sir,

We must apologise for not replying earlier to your letter with regard to the boy Cooper. We were, however, making a search for any document which would have given you a clue to the identity of the boy. It is quite true that we had a boy of the name Cooper who was employed on our S/S "Rosewood". He was afterwards transferred to our S/S "Harlseywood", and we are under the impression that he deserted this vessel somewhere in the U.S. How he eventually got back to Algiers we cannot say. The address which we had of his father was Galata, Constantinople, and we understood his father was employed in the Imperial Ottoman Bank at that port. However, when the boy deserted we wrote to his father to the Bank above mentioned, but our letter was returned. The boy Adolphus Richard Cooper was apprenticed to us in December 1913. His indentures were signed by his father as surety, and witnessed by O.O. Churchill Clerk in the Imperial Ottoman Bank, Galata, Constantinople. The boy signed the Indentures at Swansea before the Shipping Federation.

We are very sorry we have no photograph of the boy nor can we give you any letters showing signatures to identify him.

If we can supply you with any further information we shall be very pleased to do so.

> *Yours faithfully,*
> *For Constantine & Pickering Steamship Co.*
> *F.W.Murray.*

A birth certificate was obtained from Somerset House in London and this was translated before being sworn as correct by a French Magistrate. Sir Edwin Pears, the eminent solicitor and author, was yet again called upon to assist and he was able to testify that Legionnaire Debruin and Adolphus Cooper was one and the same person.

According to Edwin Pears, Arthur Cooper and his immediate family were currently on route for Messina in Sicily where Arthur had secured a post with Sanderson and Son, exporters of essential oils. Dick's older brother, Wilf, had joined the British Army and was somewhere in Egypt. He was surprised to hear that his sister Daisy had chosen to remain in Turkey.

Sitting quietly in his room at the Consulate, Dick digested the news of his family with a great deal of sadness. There seemed little doubt that his father was no more concerned about the welfare of his youngest son than he had been when the child was shipped to England. Memories of his sister, Daisy, flitted through his mind. He should have been there, with her. Did Wilf manage to visit them all? His head was reeling with so many thoughts and so many questions. He brushed away a tear as it trickled down his cheek and he realised that his face was wet from the tears that had fallen unnoticed.

Gaining his feet the boy stood smartly to attention. 'I am a Legionnaire,' he told himself. Drawing himself up to his full height he declared 'For Good Conduct Under Fire!'

Christmas 1915 was spent with the Scratchlys and soon afterwards Dick was once again on route for the Legion headquarters at Sidi-Bel-Abbes. Before leaving Bone the boy paid a last visit to his benefactors, the Mairs at St Cloud. Mr. Mair presented their young friend with a personally signed, marked copy of the New Testament which remains with me now some ninety years later, as I sit and recall the amazing facts of my father's life.

The final details required to secure Dick's discharge from the Legion was the name of the last member of his family to be born in the British Isles. Fortunately the family tree was distinguished and consequently it was simple to establish that his great-grandfather, Samuel, was born in Ireland in 1802. At the time of his birth, Samuel's father Austin owned Abbeville House which, many years later, became the home of an Irish Prime Minister, Charles Haughey. Further details of this branch of the Cooper family, who moved to Ireland from England in 1661, can be found in 'Burke's Irish Families' or, as once stated quite accidentally by my young daughter Lori, 'in that book of Irish Burkes'. I would add that this has remained a family, now shared, joke throughout the years.

Notification of his discharge from the French Foreign Legion by Ministerial Decision No 889 2/1 E was given to Dick on 25th January 1916, a month before his 17th birthday. His enlistment in October 1914 was annulled on the grounds that he had been under the legal age. They could not however annul his entitlement to the Croix de Guerre and this was attributed to him under his real name.

Following the instructions given to him by the Vice-Consulate, Dick returned to Bone expecting to be shipped from there to see his father. Issuing him with a British passport, Mr. Scratchly gave the boy some devastating news. His destination was not Sicily but Cardiff and another ship belonging to Constantine and Pickering.

With little choice in the matter, Dick joined the Hutton-wood at Cardiff and by 2nd March 1916 was transferred to the Toftwood at Penarth Dock. Although he refused to admit it, the boy was still suffering giddy spells and it was lucky that during a particularly sever attack of giddiness he pitched into the ship's hold rather than overboard.

Unconscious, he was taken by ambulance to the Royal Hamadryad Seaman's Hospital where he was examined by the Medical Superintendent, John Hartigan. Convinced his patient was suffering from shell shock, Dr. Hartigan kept the boy in hospital for several weeks under close observation.

With his usual enthusiasm and zest for life, Dick was soon making his way round the wards, chatting to everyone in sight. Noticing his patient's linguistic skills, Dr. Hartigan insisted Dick accompany him on his rounds where he could harness the boy's zeal and at the same time use his talent as an interpreter.

It was the middle of May when Dick finally left the hospital for lodgings provided for him at the local seaman's home. Still convinced that he had never been ill, there could be no question of him ever returning to the hospital under his own steam. For nine weeks he waited to be assigned to a ship and in the meantime Dr. Hartigan wrote the following letter to Arthur Cooper:-

2nd June 1916

Dear Mr. Cooper,

Your son does not *suffer from Epilepsy. The fits from which he suffers are hysteriform, undoubtedly caused by shell shock, and will, I am certain, eventually pass off. For two years after a fit it would be dangerous for him to pursue any occupation in which he was liable to serious injury during an attack. The cause of his admission to Hospital was a fall into the hold of a ship. Another such accident might be fatal.*

Everyone who meets your boy is interested in him and I am sure he will soon obtain a suitable and safe occupation. It will give me great pleasure to do anything I can for him.

> *Sincerely yours*
> *John Hartigan*

Unsure what to do about the boy, Constantine and Pickering paid him a stand-by rate for several weeks and then, suddenly, discharged him. Dick was forced to leave the Seaman's Home and for a while he wandered the streets of Cardiff during the day, sleeping in disused railway trucks at night. Destitute, he knew he must move on but before setting off he sent an unstamped letter to his father explaining he was heading for Swansea.

The forty-five mile journey to Swansea took several days and he was grateful for the food offered to him by farmers in exchange for a few odd jobs about the farms. The weather was good and he was able to sleep under hedgerows in comparative comfort eventually arriving in Swansea early in August 1916.

Meanwhile, Arthur had received the unstamped letter from his son and, putting pen to paper, vented his anger on Robert Constantine, head of the shipping company. Referring to his son the man wrote:-

'He may, for what I know, be at this hour dead with starvation.'

The letter finally concluded:-

'I also warn you that I expect an answer to the present within a fortnight from the date of its reception by you.'

Undoubtedly, if Dick was not 'at this hour dead with

starvation,' he might well have been by the time the correspondence went back and forth.

Fortunately Dick was not relying on help from anyone and was, as usual, busy fending for himself. Arriving at the docks he had managed to obtain work as a coal trimmer on the S.S.Varezze from Genoa which was heading home. Was it only a couple of years ago that he had sailed into Genoa on the Fiora? Reflecting upon happier days Dick was startled when someone shouted out his name. As he turned he was already smiling, having recognised the distinctive accent of Habanero, cook on the Fiora and now, on the S.S.Varezze.

Their arrival in Genoa was uneventful and Dick signed off the ship and said his farewells to Habanero. He was determined to seek out his family for himself, by now convinced that his father really wanted to see him. Time and distance had persuaded him that Arthur would be delighted to see his youngest son after an absence of four and a half years.

Initially mistaking surprise for delight, Dick was deliriously happy to be with his father, stepmother and stepsister. The boy was so busy hugging them and talking nineteen to the dozen that he failed to notice the cool reserve in the steely eyes of his father. That night Dick fell into a makeshift bed in the salon and slept the dreamless sleep of the innocent.

The next morning he was roused from his slumbers by his stepsister, Hetty, and together they cleared the room before the coffee pot was set on the table by his stepmother. Minutes later Arthur stormed into the room waving some letters above his head and glaring at Dick as though the boy was personally responsible for the offending correspondence.

Indirectly, he was! The letters were in reply to the threats Arthur had made to Robert Constantine.

Robert Constantine had written from West Bute Dock in

Cardiff. The letter was dated 4th September 1916.

Dear Sir,

I am in receipt of your most extraordinary letter about your son.

I have passed this on to the Owners at Middlesbro and no doubt you will be hearing from them direct.

Yours truly.
Robert Constantine

The letter from the steamship company ran into two pages in which they referred to the fact no one had disclosed *'that the poor boy was subject to fits'*. The letter went on:-

'Perhaps you will remember that we put ourselves to considerable trouble to get this boy released from the French Army, and that we have incurred a large expense in repatriating and keeping him here. We however do not complain of this, but regret that you and those responsible for his welfare should not have taken a greater interest in the boy.

We shall be glad to have a letter from you withdrawing your charges, as they are most unpleasant. The threats you make are not justified, and you make yourself amenable for the statements you have made, unless you have properly verified them.'

Needless to say it was a miserable month that Dick spent in the bosom of his family and it was with great relief that he caught a ferry back to the mainland. His future undecided and destination unknown!

8 Hazardous

He was gazing across the straits at the fast approaching mainland, desperately blinking back unshed tears. Seventeen year olds do not cry, he told himself sharply. For the first time he had honestly admitted to himself that his father really did not give a damn about him. Arthur Cooper would not care if his youngest son were to live or die. It made no difference to the man that the boy was a decorated hero, that others admired him. Dick was alone and, thinking back, realised he had been alone since that fateful day when Lucy had slipped beneath the waves in the stormy Sea of Marmara.

Where now? Dick made his way up the boot of Italy to Rome. Many lonely hours were spent wandering in the Vatican and the Lateran Museum furthering his education. Finally he continued his journey to Genoa. The weather was beautiful and the view of the Mediterranean was breathtaking in its shades of blues and gold. Somehow that filled the boy with an even greater sadness as there was no one with whom he could share such beauty. Thoughts of Lucy were persistent as, in his mind, he heard her voice as she sang the melodious Greek lullaby. He was drowning in loneliness and desperately struggled with his thoughts, seeking he knew not what!

Hours later, lounging in the shade of a peach tree, Dick was no nearer to a deciding his future than he had been on the ferry from Messina. Suddenly his siesta was disturbed by the sounds of marching feet as along the Piazza de Ferrari paraded a column of men of the Italian Alpine Regiment. As he looked, he could see comradeship, security and a few square meals to boot.

He felt no allegiance to anyone. His home was where he hung his hat. There were so many countries, so many places and so many languages. It was his duty to himself to survive and that he was determined he would do. Gaining strength from his own determination he glanced up towards heaven, the place where he knew Lucy to be, and grinning from ear to ear he gave a cheeky wink before heading down the Via Venti Settembre and into the recruiting office.

Giving his name as Arturo Riccardo Cavallaro, Dick explained he was a twenty year old Sicilian from Messina. It was amazing just how much information the boy picked up and retained from his travels. Knowing that all records had been destroyed in Messina during the 1908 earthquake gave him just the excuse he needed for not having a birth certificate.

The only person to give Dick a second glance and to query his background was a Captain Gian Battista Mascagni, said to be related to the composer of Cavalleria Rusticana, Pietro Mascagni. The Captain insisted that the accent of his newest recruit was that of a Tuscan rather than a Sicilian. With a shrug of his shoulders, Dick was secretly very pleased with the remark as the Tuscan accent was, at that time, said to be the best of spoken Italian.

The initial training was arduous if brief and after just three short weeks the battalion was off, crossing Italy for the Gorizia front. They marched the first stretch to Pontedecimo then travelled by train to Milan, on to Verona and then to Udine, seat of the Italian Commando Supremo - GHQ. Their destination was Cormons; facing Austrians entrenched on the slopes of Monte Corada.

At Udine, built on a hill some eighty miles from Venice, they packed mules for a trek up precarious mountain paths on the edge of the Italian Alps. When they made camp that night after sunset, the temperature in the mountains had plummeted and Dick was frozen. Stamping his feet, he headed further up the path trying to exercise some warmth into his body. Experience had taught him to carry his carbine at all times and when he suddenly fell on the mountainside, it was the sound of his gun firing as it hit the ground that alerted the camping soldiers to his accident.

As he fell, a bush held him for an instant before surrendering him to a yawning abyss. Semi-conscious, his hands clutched wildly at the other bushes before he was knocked out.

Dick had fallen some forty feet down a sheer rock face. A large boulder had halted his plunge and he was lying on a sloping ledge some fifty feet wide. Beyond the ledge the mountainside dropped away steeply for hundreds of feet.

It was Captain Mascagni who organised the search and when they found the fallen carbine and subsequently its owner, it was the Captain who decided that rescue would have to wait until daylight. In the meantime, medical orderlies made the descent to administer first-aid. Dick had broken his left arm above the elbow and his face was a mass of cuts, torn open by the vicious thorns of the indigenous bushes.

The next morning Dick was hauled to safety up the mountain. Back at the camp, Captain Mascagni waved the boy's British Passport under his nose.

"I will be making a full report about your accident and your identity. In the meantime you will be taken down for treatment."

The casualty clearing station was established in the Villa Sdrausina, owned by an Austrian Count, situated at Gradisca close to the Isonzo river. From the villa he was taken by ambulance to the hospital at Palmanova.

'Palmanova,' 'Palmanova!' Dick kept on repeating the name. 'Palmanova!' Why was the name so familiar to him? Each time he repeated it, he felt particularly happy as though he was about to receive a special present, a surprise. The feeling just would not go away.

The ambulance duly deposited him at the hospital doors and after a short wait, his arm was set and he was taken to the ward. Exhausted by recent events and the after effects of the anaesthetic, Dick slept for hours. Eventually his slumbers were disturbed by an uncanny feeling that he was being watched. Slowly he opened his eyes. Yes, he was right. There, standing at the foot of his bed, was a nurse clutching his chart and gazing at him with her mouth wide open.

As Dick smiled at his visitor, she looked quickly back at the chart and then, her face a picture of bewilderment, back at him. "Good evening."

She had spoken in Italian but there was no mistaking the voice. "Lucia, Lucia Valiani!" The delight in Dick's voice echoed around the ward.

"Adolphus? I thought it was you! Why Cavallaro and what are you doing here?" Lucia stopped for breath and gave him a brief glimpse of her enchanting smile.

On his discharge from the hospital, Dick stayed at the home of the Valianis where he was welcomed like a long lost son. They had heard from their daughter's school about the escapade on the pier at Worthing. Fortunately, they chose to believe Lucia's story of the events and were eternally grateful to the young lad for saving her that day from the ferocity of the sea.

Lucia's family ran the local hotel and restaurant, in better times catering mainly for the tourist trade. At the moment trade varied from the occasional short stay of a businessman to the long-term visits of military personnel.

For a while Dick helped out with the general chores, grateful for a chance to repay the kindness of his hosts. He saw for himself the incredible fight put up by the Italians on the Gorizia front. Every day wounded men were brought down from the mountains. Others made an attempt to punch a hole in the Austrian bridgehead, across the Isonzo river.

Effectively barred from fighting within the ranks of the Italian army, Dick began to strain at the leash, wanting to support the cause and fight for Italy. Seeing himself as a mud caked knight in khaki, he thought about fighting as a freelance. Eventually he parted from Lucia and her family, making for Paris and the British Army recruiting office in the Place de l'Opera.

Shortly before his eighteenth birthday and using his real name, Dick enlisted in the British Army and was instructed to report to Le Harve. Before leaving the capital he paid a visit to the French War Office obtaining written consent to wear his French medals on his British uniform. As he left the War Office a member of staff observed, "You must be very proud of your Croix de Guerre particularly as it is listed as the first to be awarded."

Dick was sent to England for basic training. At the Hampshire Barracks in Winchester, he was kitted out with his new uniform. From there he was drafted to Chisledon, near Devizes. It was during this period of training that he volunteered as an 'interpreter of the Italian language' for General P. D. Hamilton and General Delme-Radcliffe.

On 6th April 1917 Dick reported to General Hamilton at the Tower of London. He was instructed to travel the following morning with an advance party from Victoria Station to new headquarters at Gradisca. Once again he was to retrace his footsteps, this time to prepare for a large delivery of six-inch and nine-point-two-inch howitzer guns.

With a final gasp of steam, the train ground to a noisy halt in the busy Gare du Nord. Dick was to organise the transportation of luggage across Paris to the Gare de Lyon ready for the next stage of the journey. The task proved particularly easy to such a seasoned traveller and the officers were duly impressed with No 157750 Gunner Cooper of the Royal Garrison Artillery, the latest of tags for young Dick.

The Italian people were delighted to welcome British troops on their soil and as the train pulled into Turin station a friendly demonstration was in full swing.

"*Viva l'Inghilterra*! *Viva Tommy*!" came the joyful cheers.

"*Viva l'Italia*!" the soldiers shouted back.

Doors were wrenched open and the soldiers were carried from the station on the shoulders of the crowd. Eventually good-humoured policemen intervened and they were able to retrieve the luggage before being escorted to the Hotel Sitea.

The Turin episode was wholeheartedly repeated in Milan, although Dick managed to avoid a second good-natured pummelling by jumping trackside from the train.

Their arrival in Gradisca was an anti-climax after the excitement of the journey. Quietly they installed themselves in a large house, set aside for other ranks. The officers were luxuriously billeted in a nearby villa.

A conference was held at G.H.Q. Udine and, as a result, their guns were set up on the San Marco and Gorizia fronts. As the official interpreter, Dick was instructed to recruit Italian civilians to help at British Headquarters.

Cadging a lift on the back of a clangorous motorcycle, Dick directed the Italian driver to the home of Lucia Valiani in Palmanova. Killing two birds with one stone, he could spend time with Lucia while recruiting suitable personnel using the local knowledge of her family.

Once again the youngster proved his worth and provided British H.Q. with a number of mechanics, cooks, gardeners and general labourers. Few would see the age of sixty again but none could doubt their willingness to help the war effort.

All too soon his work was completed and after saying a sorrowful farewell to Lucia and her family, Dick was travelling to Rouen. The powers that be had posted the boy to serve with the 8th Gloucesters and before long he was on route for Albert, beyond Armiens.

By the 6th December 1917, Dick was on active duty in Cambrai. The weather had been dreadful and suddenly a blanket of fog draped itself heavily on to the war zone. Occasionally a shot could be heard in the distance and a muffled voice would call for directions but, on the whole, an eerie silence drifted across the region with the fog.

Dick had been on his way for supplies and before long became lost somewhere between the main trench and a small coppice of trees on the outskirts of St. Simon. Stopping to get his bearings, the boy froze as he heard heavy breathing nearby. "Don't worry, I'm on your side!"

As he swung on his heel, Dick saw a sergeant of the Royal Army Ordinance Corps and standing behind him, a terrified medic who appeared to be shaking from head to toe.

"Let's head for cover!" snapped the sergeant.

Keeping close, they ran a zigzag path as they sought refuge from stray bullets. By now they had crossed no-man's-land and were inadvertently behind enemy lines.

As the disoriented group entered the village of St. Simon they realised their mistake. Initially the place appeared deserted but German voices sent them diving for cover.

Minutes later the three soldiers were running silently in single file, dodging in and out of doorways, skirting piles of rubble. Eventually the sergeant stopped by a broken window indicating that they should enter the building. Dick needed no further bidding and was over the sill in a flash, smiling as he realised they had chosen a cafe for their shelter. Suddenly the war took on a rosy aspect as the refugees downed a particularly good champagne. At least they considered it to be particularly good!

Unexpectedly there was the deafening sound of a bomb or shell and the building opposite collapsed. Without a word the three men grabbed as many bottles as they could carry, apparently oblivious of their own skins in a desperate bid to save the booze.

The medic, heading for an inner room, tripped over the handle of a trap in the floor. Hastily they hauled the heavy timber frame revealing a perfect shelter. A sturdy ladder gave access to a dry and well stocked cellar. Smoked hams hung from blackened beams and a pair of three-hundred-litre barrels of wine stood majestically on stone plinths in adjacent alcoves. Around the walls were shelves, groaning under the weight of bottles filled with every imaginable wine and spirit.

Even heaven on earth needed some form of organisation in wartime and so Dick was hastily dispatched aloft to retrieve the forgotten rifles. He was about to cross the cafe floor when the sound of German voices had him dropping to his knees. Quietly he crawled across the room picking up one gun at a time and lowering it to his comrades below.

As they became used to the murky light in the cellar, they detected a couple of vents. As they closed them, the war seemed to drift away with only an occasional shell followed by the slow rumble of falling bricks and mortar.

Three festive British Tommies were holding an impromptu party at the expense of the French, slap in the centre of German occupied territory. They lit a hurricane lamp and like every good party, the guests proceeded to introduce themselves. The medic, who went by the name of Penrose, was gaining confidence with every drink. Finally he began to warble popular tunes with a distinctly drunken slur and was promptly shouted down by his comrades. Using a jack-knife to carve chunks of ham, the sergeant introduced himself as Chris before politely offering supper to his two companions.

The cold penetrated their sleep and Dick awoke to find Chris drowning in a pool of wine beneath an open barrel tap. Arousing the sergeant from his stupor, Dick and Penrose decided to look for blankets. The trap door was stuck fast and it took more than an hour to prise the boards apart. As air rushed into the cellar so the hurricane lamp burned more brightly and three lucky Tommies took a long and deep sobering breath of fresh air.

While they had slept an onslaught by allied forces had reduced many of the surrounding buildings to rubble. The cafe counter had been blown across the room and partly blocked the trap to the cellar. The three soldiers took turns to dig themselves out, rubble falling constantly on to their heads. Eventually a tunnel was cleared through to street level and it was here they waited for the right moment to leave. Squeaking rats brushed past them to seek sanctuary in the cellar they had so recently evacuated.

As the moon escaped from behind the clouds, Chris took a quick look around; keeping low he vanished in a mountain of bricks. Before long he returned with news of the enemy. Apparently they were well ensconced in the town even to the point of singing as they marched. Penrose panicked at the news and set off on his own without as much as a goodbye.

Chris and Dick decided on caution but it took courage to return to the cellar and share it with the rats. The two men exchanged stories and took it in turns to grab moments of fitful sleep. They had decided to wait throughout the coming day and make their escape as soon as darkness fell, giving them the maximum time in which to depart.

This time it was Dick's turn to reconnoitre and he skittered across the road, dropping to his stomach as he edged over the railway line. Beyond the track was a field criss-crossed by trenches and Dick gained the nearest of these without detection. He was heading in what he believed to be the general direction of Allied lines when he heard the sound of German voices coming towards him. For a moment he froze, expecting the enemy to round the corner and confront him. Then, adrenaline pumping, he dropped face downwards on to a firing step, feigning death.

God listened to his silent prayer and his adversaries passed him by. Unnerved by the near encounter he waited for some time before retracing his steps.

The long and seemingly endless trip back to the village was made on all fours as enemy activity had heightened considerably. It was difficult to get a bearing as the skyline of St. Simon had been obliterated. Finding Chris was not going to be easy. After a while he hissed his friend's name at every likely spot until a snarl at his elbow frightened him almost to death. "Shut up you fool!" growled Chris. The warning was just in time as a party of Germans approached on foot.

This time, as they finally made their way to the railway embankment, Dick noticed the entrance to a dugout. Further exploration revealed a comparatively large area strewn with bodies dressed in German uniforms. Deep inside the dugout they found a bunk covered with blankets, a sight that quite simply released the overwhelming tiredness they had both been holding at bay. It had been a long night.

With barely a word they climbed into the bunk, side by side, holding on to their loaded rifles beneath the blankets.

A shot jerked them to their feet and they stood back to back with guns at the ready but no movement invaded their hide. Fearfully they glanced around until Dick became aware of a warm trickle of blood on his neck. "You idiot!" he yelled at Chris. "You pulled the trigger on me!"

In a mixture of horror and relief the two men stood laughing hysterically at Dick Cooper's latest brush with death.

As the sun rose, smoke drifted across the trenches from an intense artillery onslaught launched by the British. The two men pulled on their gas masks as thick sulphurous clouds billowed into their hideout. They had only just left the village in time. There came the sound of short bursts of fire from small-arms followed by the clatter of running boots. They heard voices, German voices, raised in alarm. More footsteps thudded by.

Forgetting the pain in his head, Dick peered warily from the dugout. Judging from the sounds of battle, the Germans were defending a line to the far side of the railway embankment. Unfortunately, this left him and Chris centrally placed in no-man's-land. Before they could decide on the next step, mortars were fired and a shell landed nearby.

Dick started to search the dugout feverishly and was richly rewarded by the discovery of a box of hand-grenades.

Hidden from the sight of the enemy, who had no reason to suspect their presence, the two comrades were ideally placed for an onslaught on the Germans.

They moved quickly and quietly into the trench carrying the box of grenades between them. With the adrenaline once again flowing fast, they were back into the war with a vengeance. Almost in time with each other they commenced pulling pins and lobbing grenades with alacrity. Eventually all rifle fire was silenced. Dick and Chris slid their backs down the wall of the trench and rested on their haunches. What next? The pair were gazing at each other, holding their breath, unaware of just how successful the attack had been.

Suddenly British and French troops over-ran their position with many stopping to shake their hands. They were at a point where the British 3rd Army met the 1st French Army. After being congratulated by an English major and an Indian captain, Dick was helped to the back of the lines and into a waiting ambulance. The wound to his temple left him without the need of an explanation.

With a mock salute to Chris as he climbed aboard the ambulance, Dick was taken to a casualty clearing station at Cugny, near Ham. A medical orderly stitched the wound and the boy was ordered to re-join his unit. Several rides on a variety of army vehicles took him to Bethune where the unit medical officer, taking one look at the badly infected wound, sent him to the rear for evacuation.

His injury, which had been aggravated by neglect, kept the youngster in hospital for Christmas 1917 at St Severe.

Three months later Dick was sent by train to join his unit with the 120 Labour Corps at Arras. From there he was told to report to the St. Quentin front.

A major attack by the Germans was suspected but never the less the Allies were taken by surprise at the sheer ferocity when it came. Helped by dense fog, the German advance was so fast that one by one outposts were surrounded and taken.

Following a period of fierce fighting Dick's unit had joined a Corps that had already taken up positions with the infantry near Nesle. Awaiting orders, the boy was attracted by a large house, standing on a hilltop, just outside the village.

'I bet they have a good larder', he thought. 'And probably a well stocked wine cellar'.

The house seemed to be in allied-occupied territory and nothing much seemed to be happening. Dick set off alone, zigzagging as he went as much to avoid detection by his own side as by the enemy. Misjudging the speed of the advance, just as his superiors had done, he was hit by bullets from two enemy machine guns.

He had got within thirty yards of the house and saw the spit of the guns that had been mounted just beneath the window frames. One burst of fire had crippled his right knee. Then, as he crumpled in pain, they fired again hitting his other leg.

Only semi-conscious, he managed to roll down the slope out of control but also out of the sight of his assailants.

The British artillery, alerted to the strategic position of the enemy, hastily dispatched a barrage of shells with little thought given to accuracy in their excitement.

Sick with pain and with legs paralysed, Dick rolled further down the hill in an attempt to avoid being hit by his own side. Eventually and mercifully he sank into the arms of oblivion.

9 Indomitable

The pain in his legs as he bounced up and down on a makeshift stretcher was indescribable. Thankfully consciousness came and went until, aboard a crowded ambulance, he was given painkilling injections.

All around him the world had gone mad. Hustle and bustle, soldiers walking in all directions, people on bikes, ambulances, men shouting, gun fire. He drifted into a fitful sleep and again heard the gunfire, and again, and yet again. Someone was screaming but as he dragged himself into consciousness, the screaming stopped.

Thoughts came and drifted away again. 'This time I have really done it'.

Dick was nineteen years of age, paralysed from the waist down and he knew of no one who would have sufficient interest to be told about his misfortune let alone take care of him.

The ambulances travelled in convoy to Montidier where there was a particularly long and uncomfortable wait while wagons were hitched together to form a hospital train. Hundreds of wounded men were loaded aboard to be treated en route by just two doctors. Thousands more, equally in need of help would be left behind. The situation was completely out of hand.

Luckily the ambulance driver had parked in an appropriate place so that Dick and his fellow travellers were carted on to the train. Few complained of the pain. Few complained of anything, knowing full well that they were among the most fortunate.

As the train eased its self noisily out of the sidings, dragging and banging the loaded wagons, the doctors made their rounds. The stench in the wagons told its own story of blood, sweat and tears. Injections and drinks were administered to the most critically wounded. Raising himself on his elbows, Dick began to look around with suspicion. Pain-racked bodies seemed to relax as though in death.

Terror gripped him. Euthanasia, the word banged around his brain. They are going to kill me, he muttered. I am no use and they are going to kill me. His knuckles turned white as he gripped the makeshift cot on which he lay. As a doctor approached him the boy refused the offered painkiller. He fought with the orderly who tried to make him drink water.

They had started travelling northwards but were soon turned back, the engine shunting the groaning train in reverse. Whispered messages flittered from stretcher to stretcher; the railway line had been cut just a short distance ahead.

Upon their return to Montidier, the men were quickly transferred to canal barges. Someone was obviously ahead of the problem, although room was even more limited. Once again, Dick was among the chosen. It seemed they had covered much of the canal system in northern France before finally landing in the region of Calais. All the hospitals were overflowing and consequently huge marquees had been erected adjacent to the Calais building.

At last proper examinations were made of the diverse injuries suffered by the soldiers. When Dick's turn arrived, he was already waiting for the worse possible news. He had seen the damage to his legs and was fairly sure that at least one of them would be 'for the chop'. His flippant attitude hid the terror that had turned his stomach into a block of concrete.

That evening his name went on to the operating list, his bed was moved close to the theatre and he was given a sedative, which he took this time without question.

Early the next morning Dick was taken into theatre and laid on the narrow operating table. An elderly, careworn orderly fussed around him, quickly and efficiently removing the blood-soaked bandages from his legs. The surgeon, looking equally exhausted, approached the table shaking his head. "Amputation above the knee, both legs," he added as he peered over the table.

Dick had expected the news and yet it still hit him with the force of a thunderbolt. He surprised himself with his quiet and dignified reply. "Well, if you must, you must. Yes, yes, whatever!" Inside he wanted to scream at this man, he wanted to fight, he wanted to lash out at everyone and everything around him. The concrete ball left his stomach and he felt he could leap from the table and run, and run, and run.

Instead, he closed his eyes and said a silent prayer to anyone who may listen. Then he thought of Lucy and a slight smile touched his lips for the merest speck in time.

As on so many previous occasions, some uncanny force was already at work, turning the tide in his favour. The appearance of his saviour was sudden, although the theatre staff hardly glanced at the tall distinguished-looking man who had quietly entered the room. The stranger, wearing the uniform of a French general, crossed to the table and smiled down at the young man. He started to discuss the injuries with the surgeon and Dick entered into the conversation, joining the two men in their own language.

"You are French?" asked the general.

"*Non, mon general.* I was a Foreign Legionnaire once, but now I serve with the British Army."

The two men walked away from the bed and Dick could no longer hear the conversation. He knew the General was speaking quickly, almost in excitement. The nursing staff members were still bustling busily around the room but the atmosphere had changed, the sombreness gone.

The general removed his coat, scrubbed his hands and approached the operating table with determination. "Let's see if we can save these legs, shall we?" The question was asked of no-one in particular. "Tell me if this hurts?"

The man prodded and probed, testing the youngster's reactions. Several minutes passed. Dick knew that his whole future lay in the hands of this stranger and he held his breath.

"Courage!" The General grinned while indicating to an assistant that he needed a mask.

Only later did Dick discover that his liberator had been none other than General Calmette, the eminent bacteriologist, the co-developer of the Bacillus Calmette-Guerin (B.C.G.), the vaccine used in the treatment of T.B.

The long ward was full of moving shadows and Dick became aware of a ghostly shape at his side. He wanted to look towards his legs, to look for his legs; he tried to feel if they were still there. Time and time again he awoke and drifted back to sleep. Time and time again he tried to feel for his legs. He began to think he was in a never-ending nightmare. The ghost seemed to come and go. He felt someone holding his hand and he knew it was the ghost. How could ghosts hold hands? Perhaps they did. How could anyone possibly know unless they had met one!

He heard a voice. A woman's voice! Lucy? No, Lucy was dead! Perhaps I am dead, he thought. The voice came again and this time he could make out the words. "You are well. You will get better!" The voice spoke with confidence.

"Are they still there?" He asked in French.

"Yes, you lucky boy." The words were spoken in the soft Devonshire accent of an English Red Cross nurse.

He wanted to dance, sing, to float on air. No, jump for the sheer joy of living and of having two good legs to live with. Looking down the bed he could see that a wire cage protected his legs from the weight of the army blankets. Closing his eyes, Dick gave silent thanks for his very good fortune. If General Calmette had not chosen that very moment to arrive, his legs may well have been discarded with the rubbish.

Several days passed before Dick was able to take serious stock of the situation. It would be a long and uphill haul to regain the use of his legs. It was one thing to have saved them; it was quite another to make them fully functional again. First he became obsessed with the need to wriggle his toes and beads of sweat slid down his face as he willed them into life.

His sense of humour had fully recovered and he would tease the nurses unmercifully as they unwrapped the yards of bandages from his tortured limbs. Rubber catheter tubes had been attached to his knees like narrow tentacles, to carry away the fluid. Despite his bravado, the pain was excruciating and he was given regular injections of morphine. Before long he became dependent on the drug for sleep.

Hospital beds in France were at a premium and Dick was transferred as soon as he was well enough to be moved. The journey to St. Albans, in England, was tiring in the extreme. Military transport carried him to the Napsbury Hospital, a Hertfordshire mental hospital converted to treat the war wounded. At least it is better than the last mental hospital I was in, he thought to himself wryly.

Sister Higgins, an Irish paragon, was in charge of the ward. Young Dick Cooper was taken firmly under her wing and remained her favourite patient throughout his stay. His wounds healed well in the ensuing weeks although there were days and nights when the pain was unbearable. Only morphia brought him relief and he was becoming more and more dependent on the drug.

When the inevitable instruction came to withdraw the medication the young man was distraught. Using all his wiles, Dick started watching and planning and before long established a route to the drug through an incompetent ward orderly. Obtaining morphia and a syringe he began injecting himself. Fortunately, he was not quite as clever as he thought. The doctor had expected far more trouble from his patient as a result of withdrawing the drugs and when this seemed not to be the case, he investigated and caught Dick red-handed. Luckily a rehabilitation programme was quickly put into place and Dick's craving slowly cured.

This was a young man with a strength of character far beyond his years. He had always met life head on and was not about to hide behind debilitating drugs. Substituting a mixture of determination and guts for the morphine he set about walking again. There was little more the medical team could do. The rest was up to him.

His legs, useless for so long, had to be re-educated. Crutches were duly issued and Dick would launch himself forward, on a daily adventure, like a new born foal fresh from the womb. With his back against his bed he would survey the well-scrubbed hospital floor spread invitingly before him. Then, lurching unsteadily, he was off towards freedom and the unknown. It was a major milestone when, six months after he was shot, Dick graduated to a walking stick and the world outside.

As the weeks and months had passed, General Calmette was frequently in his thoughts and he felt he should, at the very least, say thank you to the man. Eventually Dick realised that there were no words, in any of his eight languages, to aptly express his gratitude to the man who gave him back his legs. It was inevitable that wherever Dick went in life, General Calmette would walk with him. He just hoped that the General was aware of that fact.

Dick was on leave in London on 11th November 1918 when the city exploded with the Armistice Day jubilation. The celebrations went on into the night and the excitement was infectious. For Dick the festivities were just the tonic he needed, giving him the will to continue with both the treatment and the exercises to further strengthen his legs.

Fit and well at last Dick travelled to Mill Hill Camp, near Winchester. It was early in March 1919 and soldiers from all over the world were gathering at the camp prior to demobilisation. On 31st March 1919 Dick Cooper left the British Army having served a total of two and a half years. He had collected his discharge paper, form B2067, and a travel warrant to Messina. Vaguely he wondered why he had chosen Messina as his destination. He certainly had no real desire to return to Sicily. Eventually he decided that his choice had been due to a lack of suitable alternatives.

Twenty years of age, footloose and fancy free, Dick set off at snail's pace to cross France heading in the general direction of Sicily. A diversion to Marseilles was inescapable and as he stood gazing across the picturesque harbour, memories of happier days floated in with the evening tide.

Enjoying the warmth of the sun as he ambled down the steps of the Gare St. Charles, Dick heard a friendly shout. Turning to the sound of the voice, he saw Al Roberts heading towards him at a gallop. "Hi there, slow up you old bounder!" He greeted the former corporal with a grin. They had served together at Caserne Trupel, Rouen, and would have a lot of catching up to do over a few glasses of the local wine.

The British Army was returning from Egypt and the Near East through Marseilles and a large transport depot had been established at the local abattoir. There were sixty or seventy lorries in use, mostly Leylands, being driven by Frenchmen. A Captain was in charge of the military staff, who were few in number and worked either in the office or on maintenance. Al had managed to get himself a job at the depot as a civilian worker and he persuaded Dick to put in an application and join him.

The work involved issuing work chits to civilians and explaining their duties. At the end of each day he compared the scheduled journeys with the recorded mileage, in an attempt to eliminate petrol frauds. Nevertheless petrol disappeared at an alarming rate. So did tyres. The magnetos of a dozen Daimler cars, kept at the depot, vanished overnight. Eventually the Daimlers themselves were spirited away. Next on the list was the lorries and it was evident that no one knew or cared what was going on. Certainly someone was making a very nice profit and it was not the British.

By the time the depot closed, Dick had saved some of his wages for a holiday. This was a new concept for him and he was extremely proud of himself. He decided that Nice would be an excellent destination and managed to hitch a lift along the coast with one of the local lorry drivers.

Days later, having sampled the delights of Nice, he headed for Monte Carlo. The fascination of the Casino beckoned him to the tables and beginners' luck favoured him for a while. Within a week he had won thousands of pounds but Lady Luck, ever the fickle mistress, turned her attention elsewhere and he began to lose. He tried doubling and trebling his stakes in a vain bid to re-coup his losses. In a matter of days his capital had dwindled to a few francs, just enough to pay his fare back to Marseilles and reality.

Reaching the port of Marseilles was one thing, but what now? For several hours he kicked around the old haunts until he found himself seated on the stone wall skirting the Fort St

Jean. Inside he would find food, shelter and friends. The sun sprayed silver streaks on the gently rippling sea as a boat moved slowly out of the harbour. Memories flooded over him, Messina, Constantinople, Worthing, Cardiff, and inevitably, the Sea of Marmara.

Dragging himself to his feet, Dick rounded the building until he came face to face with a sentry in the big gateway. The man made no move to stop him, but he smiled knowingly as Dick sauntered past him. The guard was wearing his kepi visor broken to form an inverted V over his forehead so he was obviously a veteran.

More smiles were in evidence as Dick entered the guardroom to report. He was perplexed.

"Anyone here know me?" He asked, thinking that could account for his reception.

An old campaigner, who was sitting in the corner smoking, pointed a nicotine stained finger in the direction of the newcomer. "Come to re-join, have you?"

Dick was puzzled until the smoker added. "Don't worry, Legionnaire is written all over you. You have the gait, the nonchalance, that proud air. Yes, you are a Legionnaire alright!"

It was 8th July 1919 and he was twenty years and four months old. A couple of scribbled signatures put him back into the ranks of the French Foreign Legion for a minimum period of five years.

That night, lying on a wooden slatted bunk, Dick gave some thought to the fighting force to which he had returned so willingly. The majority of Legionnaires were men of fine character, staunch, brave and loyal. Men who joined the Legion for a variety of reasons including the love of adventure and physical danger. Whatever it was that sent these men from their homelands, from the love of women, from civilisation, the Legion could help. In some mysterious way, life in the French Foreign Legion would obliterate the scars of the past.

Whatever his character, however much he grumbled, after a year or so the Legionnaire would become imbued with the spirit of the Legion and most of them, even the mutinous, would find what they came for: a quiet conscience, forgetfulness, regeneration of character, or death.

Of course there were some who would never make the grade, the anti-social, the unrepentant criminal, hopeless cases who had no intention of conforming. These men posed a danger to themselves and to the men with whom they served.

These were early days for Dick and being recognised as an 'old stager' he was expected to know all the rules. No allowances were made for him. Soon he came to realise that soldiers of the Legion in peacetime bore no resemblance to the hell-hole fighters of Gallipoli.

An adventurer since birth, Dick found the boredom suffocating. Cleaning, polishing and marching were activities to which he could not relate. Soon he began to realise that he had made a terrible mistake. Conditions were just not the same and the comradeship of war was missing altogether. For a while the French Foreign Legion had been his home, the Legionnaires his brothers. He had returned, seeking his past, forgetting the former horrors, remembering only the good times.

During the first three months at the Legion's headquarters in Sidi-Bel-Abbes Dick was reckless and insubordinate. The constant feeling of being tested, reminded him of his father and just served to raise the devil in him. He obeyed orders only when it suited him to do so. When he felt inclined, he missed roll calls. Before long he was in serious trouble, reported by the sergeant for 'habitual insubordination,' he was sentenced to sixty days imprisonment.

In the prison, each man was confined to a cell so narrow that it was impossible to take one pace across it. The length of about four paces was mostly taken up by a slab on which to sleep. In the corner of the room stood a tin utensil, providing basic en suite facilities for the occupant. The winter was severe but even in the coldest weather only one blanket was issued to the inmates. Overcoats were confiscated.

A lone bugler sounded Reveille at five each morning when the men were made to clean their cells. At six o'clock they were marched to a pump, set in a yard close to the staff kitchens, each waiting for their turn to wash in the freezing water. Meanwhile the smell of cooking twisted their empty stomachs into agonising knots.

Each prisoner was given a bag filled with forty kilos of sand and stones to carry and from seven-thirty to ten o'clock they marched around the prison yard. Depending on the duty guards, sometimes they were ordered to run, kneel, lie down and then get up and march again.

At 10 o'clock sharp they were sent back to their cells for the first meal of the day, cut rations. Following an hour of rest on the slabs, the prisoners were up, out, and marching with their loads until five in the afternoon. Exhausted, the weary men who by now could hardly stand, were given food and locked away for the night.

Every single day, when Dick returned from the gruelling torture, he was writhing with fury, with a burning anger that only served to remind him of his father. He would lay there on the solid slab, oblivious of the cold beneath his aching back, obsessed with his hatred of authority.

When his sixty days were served, he was marched to the colonel's office and warned that next time he would be sent to the Penal Battalion. The threat carried some weight as the reputation of the Penal Battalion was far worse than the prison at Sidi-Bel-Abbes.

Giving the matter some serious thought, Dick decided to apply for the mounted battalion, the Compagnie Montee stationed at Kenadza. On arrival, he was delighted to take charge of a small black Spanish mule called Aisha. Together they were to assist in transporting rations to the forts of southern Algeria.

Before long, Dick and Aisha were joined by a Legionnaire called Schneider, a German by birth. The three of them formed a close bond and often both men would walk all day through the burning sand to rest the mule. Aisha even shared their ration biscuits when, for just a few minutes, they sought shade from the remorseless sun.

Weeks later they were assigned to the Trans-Saharan Project, the quest for a route through the unexplored region of the Western Sahara which would open up the Niger Valley. The prospect had tantalised Europe, and notably the French, for generations. Cars and coaches now follow the trail blazed by the Legionnaires. However in 1919 they had, at best, only the age-old caravan routes to guide them. Often there were not so much as the faintest camel tracks and they were forced to make completely new paths in areas that had been without rain for years. The region was unsuitable for mules and forty camels were borrowed from the Compagnie Saharienne to carry their kit, food and water.

The first stop was Reggan, three hundred and fifty miles away. From there they travelled a further four hundred and fifty miles south to the western fringe of the mysterious Hauger (Ahaggar) Mountains, crossing the Tanezrouft Desert, known as 'The Land of Thirst'. The hardship and monotony of life in the Sahara became unbearable when Dick was forced to celebrate his twenty-first birthday in the desert.

The company returned to Kenadza and then new orders arrived, detailing the building of a road towards the Moroccan border. They were constantly opening up new country by the very sweat of their brow and hoping that, one day, history would record their efforts. The road project took them towards Djebel Sarro, on the Algerian side of the Haut Atlas Mountains. Outposts were built along the way to help with the occupation of the territory.

Then came a few months respite when Dick was sent to Sidi-Bel-Abbes to undergo a training course for corporals. The training was very thorough including both practical exercises and classroom theory. Not only did he learn the general fighting tactics of the Arabs but also the strategy employed by individual tribes in Morocco. One of the most useful exercises, in particular to serve him well in later years, was mastering several local dialects.

The course was completed successfully and Dick was drafted to the 3rd battalion of the 1st Regiment and sent south again, this time to the region of Bou Denib. There was fierce fighting in the area around Bou Denib and Erfoud and during the first week they were attacked daily. As the area settled down again, so the men were transferred and Dick spent some more time in the Sahara before being sent back to Kenadza. Here he found Schneider and with him a route to deep trouble.

Schneider was a desperate man ready to quit, knowing the only way out would be desertion. (Contrary to the popular concept, Legionnaires – like any other serving soldiers – do not and did not escape, they desert.) The officer in charge at Kenadza was a tyrant who enjoyed making life as difficult as possible for his men and Schneider couldn't take much more. Before long, Dick had become a willing participant in his friend's plan.

While serving in the Sahara boredom had been Dick's constant bedfellow and his thoughts had frequently run riot. He dreamed of the cool breezes on the mountains of Austria and Italy, the freshness of the woodland at Epping, rush of the waves pounding the pier at Worthing, and always Lucy – his beloved Lucy. The restlessness had grown and grown, had unnerved him, until he had felt as barren as the desert region itself.

Once the thought of leaving was firmly in their heads they could not get rid of it. The more they discussed the possibility the more real it became. A new adventure! They would have to cross hundreds of miles of sand and the Plateau de Tel to reach the northern coast of Morocco. It was a stiff proposition. On reaching the coast, if they made it that far, they would have to make their way down to Tangiers, the international port.

They planned for days, frequently arguing about the details. Eventually, they agreed it would be safer to disguise themselves as Arabs and they set about collecting suitable clothing. Their naturally dark hair with skin tanned by the desert sun gave the idea credence. It was shortly after mid-night when two shabbily dressed Arabs finally left the barracks to head northwards into the desert.

Their capture at Meridja was so fast that they had no time to enjoy any fruits of freedom. Dick was in serious trouble being faced with the Penal Battalion. They were awaiting ratification of his sentence when the Battalion was ordered to march. With nothing to lose, the two men decided to make a second attempt at deserting.

This time they took the planning more seriously. To be caught a second time was unthinkable. This time it really had to work. The first step was to carefully map the route, establishing the whereabouts of watering places. They gave a great deal of thought to their disguises finally coming up with the idea of dressing as Spanish beggars, of which there were many in Morocco. Schneider even managed to purloin a battered old accordion to add authenticity to the story.

Eventually, as two shabby 'Spaniards,' they left Kenadza and started northwards through the desert. Fear of capture had them travelling by night and going into hiding during daylight. Inevitably hunger got the better of them and it became necessary to go into an Arab village to beg. Much to his surprise Dick discovered that Schneider really could play the accordion. It had not occurred to him to ask before, considering the instrument to be nothing more than a prop. At the village they managed to earn a few francs, some olives and a little bread.

Misfortune struck on the following day when Dick developed a severe attack of malaria. They had no choice but to lie up for a few days and Schneider had his work cut out in trying to keep his friend quiet. Constantly Dick was shouting out in a state of delirium. The German spent the days at his friend's side and the nights fetching water and what little food he could find. The illness reached crisis point and gradually began to abate until a smiling young man cheekily asked, "What are we waiting for?"

The deserters marched night after night through the sand and over rocks until they had worn through the soles of their boots. They used the northern star to guide them through the darkness and occasionally they travelled in the day when they used Marabous, holy places of which the doors faced Mecca, to find their way.

Approaching the Plateau de Tel, the going became exceedingly tough. Now and then they would stop at a village and the German would play traditional songs from home to keep them in food. According to their calculations they were getting close to Ain Sefra. Suddenly, Schneider dropped to his knees, incapable of taking another step. The man had gone down with malaria and it took all Dick's strength to drag his friend into the shade of some palm trees. There was nothing that could be done except wait until the fever broke. The German was dreadfully ill, violently delirious. As luck would have it water was close by and Dick found dates to keep himself going while he soothed his friend's fevered brow.

At last they were free to move again, the illness going almost as quickly as it had arrived. It was essential to find food and they headed towards the Atlas Mountains and the village of Talsint, inhabited by the Ahmed ou Said tribe.

The village was guarded by a pack of about ten dogs. Baring their fangs, the animals bounded from the palm trees as the strangers approached. Dick squatted on his heels quietly telling his friend to do the same. As the dogs came close, Dick spoke to them softly in Arabic. They stopped in their tracks but continued to bark lustily. Again Dick spoke to them, giving them names and trying various Arab dialects.

One of the animals reminded him of Osman and so he called him gently by that name. The dog slithered towards him on his stomach and the others followed suit, lolling their heads and pricking up their ears as though understanding every word. Soon they were wagging their tails in open friendship.

Veiled women, who met them on the village outskirts, were surprised to see the dogs making a fuss of infidels. Questions came from all sides. Who were they? Where did they come from? A scruffy young man pulled himself up to his full height and said. "I am an Ottoman from the old Turkish Empire." With a wink at his German companion, Dick smiled as the Arabs bowed their heads in reverence at his mention of those once all-powerful rulers.

A feast was prepared in their honour, with the usual dishes of couscous and roast lamb, accompanied by green tea. As they ate it was impossible not to notice the emaciated state of the Arab children and they winced at the sight of flies swarming over abscesses on the children's faces and bodies.

Good manners dictated they finish the meal but immediately afterwards Dick set about treating the children's ailments. He took off his tattered shirt and tore it into bandages, asking his friend to do the same. They managed to organise the villagers to boil water and gradually they dealt with the children's sores. The Arabs were impressed that these men should show such concern for their children and they gave Dick the name of 'toubib,' doctor.

There was little doubt that the toubib and his friend were welcome to stay as long as they wished but the men realised that these people could not afford to feed two extra mouths. Avoiding emotional farewells, Dick and Schneider left the village a few days later under the cover of darkness.

In the way of the desert, their fame went before them and at each tribal encampment they were received with open arms. "Salaam, toubib," the Arabs greeted them. With touching faith they brought their sick to the healer and it staggered Dick to see how much an elementary knowledge of medicine could help these simple folk. The most common complaints were infected eyes and wounds. Some of the babies were victims of primitive circumcision. Hygiene was unknown in that part of the world and wounds were left to become septic and fly infested simply out of ignorance. Sickness and disease were crosses to bear rather than enemies to fight.

All Dick could do was bathe the sores and wounds in boiled water, apply poultices where necessary and bandage with any clean linen he could find.

Eventually the two friends returned to their deception and headed again for Ain Sefra. Their disguise was now complete as they both had bushy beards to hide their faces from prying eyes. For the first time they risked going among Legionnaires and Europeans. They were the very last word in tatterdemalion beggardom. Dick's Spanish stood them in good stead and Schneider remembered to keep his mouth shut.

From Ain Sefra they walked to Saida and then, branching left, headed for Morocco and the sea. Travelling became quicker as by now they were able to hitch lifts on lorries and carts. By the time they reached Tlemcen, the journey had taken seven weeks and covered a distance of five hundred kilometres. They were beginning to feel safe, reasonably sure of success.

They were still visiting cafes and bars and Dick collected the takings while Schneider played the accordion to his hearts content. Confident in their ability to deceive, they went to the European establishments seeking richer pickings. More money meant a big mistake in the guise of local wine. It had been a long time since they had celebrated anything and so it wasn't long before they were both well and truly drunk.

As Dick awoke in the bowels of the military prison at Oran he realised that seven weeks of torture had provided him with nothing more than a beard and blisters.

10 Judgement

Colomb Bechar stood alone in the arid desert. There were no barracks in the Penal Battalion, the prisoners all living under canvas. It was from Colomb Bechar that most of the horror stories of the French Foreign Legion originated. Known as the Compagnie de Discipline, it was composed of two sections, the Section Ordinaire and the Section de Repression, the names speaking for themselves.

Dick and Schneider were separated and their boots were removed each night to discourage them from any further desertion.

Initially men were attached to the Section de Repression where talking and smoking was not allowed. The work amounted to hard labour with quarrying and brick-making being the two main operations. Dick was set to work in a group of five, making bricks with straw and clay for the building of mechtas, the Arab houses.

The men communicated with each other by the occasional grin, a shake of the head, a nod, a wink and a wave. The vast majority of the prisoners were smokers and the absence of cigarettes put them under far more strain than the hard work. Alternatively, the hard work served to keep their hands busy.

The sergeants, who were not chosen for their gentle natures and their kind hearts, ran the battalion. These men enjoyed inflicting punishment on others. Dick, like the other prisoners, viewed the hierarchy with great respect and tried to avoid any confrontational situations, knowing that he would lose every time. It was unfortunate when, without thinking, he stooped to retrieve a half-smoked cigarette lying on the ground before him. He was too new to realise this was no more than a trick instigated by one of the guards. As he retrieved the cigarette, a whip was brought down on his back with such force that he fell to his knees before his reflexes had him springing forwards with fists ready to deal with his attacker. The man next to him grabbed for his arm and spun him in his tracks, trying to save Dick from further punishment. Even so, his yielding to temptation earned him fifteen days imprisonment.

As the young man was dragged away he gave a sardonic smile, realising he was about to be imprisoned while in prison. Well, I can't have much further than this to go, he thought in defiance.

Then he discovered the meaning of imprisonment, Colomb Bechar style. Dick was made to dig a grave and then to lie in it on his back. A small piece of canvas was then stretched over the hole, supposedly to protect the inmate from the sun but, invariably, this was left at a discreet angle thereby ensuring the sun bought further misery throughout the day.

On rare occasions the prisoner was fed dried bread and a minimum of water. At one time he was left to the point of starvation and then tempted with a metal container of soup. Dick could see bits of meat in the soup and even the grease floating on the top looked appetising. Grabbing the tin hungrily, he gulped at the meat and gravy. Only when he had finished the meal did he realise the fluid had been pure brine, so salty that he thought he would vomit. Very soon the intended torment of an intolerable thirst threatened to drive him insane. Constantly he begged for water that was refused each time with a laugh from the sentry. That evening more soup was brought to him. This time he tasted it warily and found it to be even saltier than before. The guard who had brought this latest repast was gazing down into the hole with an evil smile twisting his features, establishing that he was gaining personal perverted pleasure from the torture being inflicted on the prisoner. Hatred of the man welled up inside Dick as he leapt from the grave, punching out with all the force he could muster. The man dropped like a stone but before Dick could even begin to think of escaping, he was struck from behind, a rifle butt landing behind his right ear knocking him unconscious.

Needless to say, the disciplinarians of the French Foreign Legion had not run out of ideas and the next punishment provided pure, excruciating agony. This was a discipline known as crapaudin, a specific method of tying up a man, 'crapaud' being the word for toad in French. Such contortion was achieved by throwing a man on to his stomach, dragging his legs and arms back and then tying his ankles and wrists firmly together.

Dick was left tied up all night. He was to remember that night as long as he lived, such torment being impossible to forget. Later, hours after he had been untied, the agonising pains continued in his back and across his shoulders. He was unable to move within his prison-grave and in a state of half consciousness, believed himself to be permanently paralysed.

As the days passed so the pain eased, although it was several weeks before he was to feel really fit again. Meanwhile he became more used to lying in the grave and, at times, was distracted by the antics of Schneider. His friend was risking similar punishment by defying authority and making regular trips out to the compound to feed his friend with any scraps he could obtain.

Eventually, with his time served, Dick was taken before the Captain. "Well Cooper, how are you feeling?" There was a long pause. "Have you been given a cigarette?" The man looked directly into the eyes of the delinquent before him.

The unresponsive young man was unsure as to the answers expected of him and decided it would be safer to remain silent than to say something out of place. He stood there, looking as subdued as he genuinely felt and at the same time, trying to appear interested.

The Captain obviously thought this was a man worthy of some time and effort so, instructing Dick to sit, he proceeded to talk quietly to him just as a father might talk to a son. The young man was given a great deal to think about. The meaning of pride was carefully explained, the need to have pride in oneself and in one's actions before it became possible to have pride in anything or anyone else. Dick was given a new awareness of himself as a person, as an individual who could think and act in his own best interest. He began to realise that his first duty was to himself and that he really wanted to have a good reason to hold his head high, fulfilling his own personal needs. It was not necessary to prove his worth to others, only to himself. The person in whom he could trust implicitly, the one who deserved his respect, the individual for whom he should care above all others and who, in return, would care for him was Dick Cooper. He had a future, a future of which he could be proud. At this moment his future lay within the ranks of one of the world's most respected armies, the French Foreign Legion. There would be a life beyond and to think of those years ahead brought an excitement of its own, anticipation of the unknown. It was 'his' destiny and he intended having a hand in it.

The slate could be wiped clean for him. The decision was his to make. The captain sent him away to his tent and he was given a day to reflect, to consider all his options. He lay there alone, on a mattress stuffed with esparto grass, which felt like duck's down after the solid dirt-base of his recent 'grave'. He had already made up his own mind and the first step was to have a good sleep.

The next day the captain sent for Dick and after a brief pause, during which he gave his visitor a penetrating glance, the man smiled. "Welcome, Legionnaire Cooper. Welcome!"

To ensure the newly reformed character was helped on to the right tracks, a more interesting job was found for him and Legionnaire Schneider was allowed to work with him. They were given careful training in the laying and the blowing up of explosives.

In the quarries at Colomb Bechar, it was necessary to blast out the limestone that was then burned to make the lime. Both young men took an interest in all aspects of the job, becoming familiar with the amount of charge needed, the length of Bickford cord required and the exact moment to fire it. They also worked extremely well as a team, which had been one of the aims of the captain in arranging for them to work together.

One particular day they had a total of twenty two mines to blow up before lunch and they set about laying the charges as the true professionals they had become. The holes were between five and twelve feet apart and had been filled with the charge, chedite. Working from the outside and making their way towards each other they started to fire the charges, Schneider going the faster of the two. Suddenly a mine exploded too quickly and Dick saw his friend drop. Leaving the rest of his charges, Dick raced over to where his comrade was laying motionless, reaching him just as another mine exploded, taking him with it.

When he awoke in the military hospital the feeling was undoubtedly one of deja vu. For a few moments the hushed voices took him back in time and instinctively he felt for his legs, relief flooding over him as he realised they were still there. Soon afterwards he began to feel the pain of his injuries, mainly in his legs and back but also a few to his head. As the quarry had erupted around them, stones had shot out like bullets and imbedded themselves into the two casualties. His injuries were more serious than he first appreciated and as soon as they could move him, he was transported to the hospital at Oran. During his stay in Oran, which lasted several months, Dick was granted a full pardon, thanks to an excellent report provided by the captain.

Following his recovery, Dick was transferred back to the Compagnie Saharienne, which had been divided into a number of smaller companies. The area to survey and control was vast, stretching beyond the Ahaghar Mountains to Lake Chad in French Equatorial Africa. The companies were named after the districts they patrolled. Dick was sent to the Touat Gourara Company, based on Timimoun.

Five Legionnaires, including Dick, travelled for two months by camel to reach Timimoun. All five had trades at their fingertips, upholding the proud boast that the Legion was equipped to do any job, anywhere. Each of the companies was self-supporting, even as far as making their own boots and harnesses.

The place was little more than four outer walls, a few huts and a well. The water came from a segya, or underground river, which had plunged beneath the sand some eighty or ninety miles away. They continued with their former routine, facing hectic skirmishes with bands of nomadic marauders who wandered the area killing and pillaging. Some periods were particularly dangerous, fighting an unscrupulous enemy, and others would be dull and boring when life seemed timeless.

Time and time again, Dick would isolate himself among the dunes experiencing that strange feeling of being alone and yet, a part of something he did not understand. It was as though something had entered his very soul and he was in touch with nature herself: passions, sorrows, ambitions, hardships, all would fade into insignificance. At such moments a man is perhaps nearer to 'the peace of God which passeth all understanding' than at any other time until he comes to die.

Completing his five years of service in 1924, Dick decided to visit his sister Daisy. They hadn't met since the day he had left Constantinople in 1912, but she had written to him recently with the news she was to be married. The wedding was to be in Paris, which seemed an ideal place to renew the relationship with his sister and with the great world outside.

Once in the French capital, Dick was completely lost. It was so long since he had spoken with civilians that he seemed to have lost the ability to communicate. The wedding was a quiet affair, attended by a few relations on both sides, with the exception of their parents! A matter of days after the nuptials, the blissful couple planned to return to Constantinople and Dick decided to accompany them for part of the way. Trying, as always, to establish a common meeting ground with his father, Dick had decided to retrace his steps to Messina.

The first stage of their journey took them by train to Lyon, where they were to stay with some of the groom's relations for a few days. The members of the Devaurieaux family were proud to welcome Raoul's brother-in-law to their home and were enthralled by some of the tales the young man could tell of his exploits abroad.

Romance was in the air and having spent many hours with the newly weds, and with love being the most infectious of conditions, Dick's resistance to matrimony was seriously weakened. It was inevitable that a beautiful girl should arrive on the scene at exactly the right moment. Simone was dark haired and dark eyed with huge dimples in both cheeks. She was the groom's third cousin by marriage and her laughter could be heard in every room of the house.

Dick fell head over heels in love with the girl and in a matter of days he had proposed marriage and, to his amazement, had been accepted. The next step was to obtain permission for the wedding from Simone's father. This daunting prospect was postponed until Dick returned from Marseilles where he was due to see Daisy and Raoul off to Constantinople.

As he waved goodbye to the happy pair, wedded bliss departed with them. Dick was horrified by his own stupidity. Simone was a lovely girl but what else did he know about her? They had only just met, what did they have in common? Was he ready to give up the wanderlust? Would it be fair to tie them both down without knowing if he could stay in one place for more than a week or two?

Instead of returning to Lyon, he travelled on to Paris. He desperately needed time to think. It occurred to the young man that if Simone were the right woman for him, he would not now be having such serious doubts. Then he realised that he was frightened stiff at the prospect of marriage to her. Quickly, he made his way to the Rue St Dominique where he signed on for a further five years in the French Foreign Legion, returning to the only real home he had known. As he wrote his name, the date struck him as an omen. It was 8th October 1924 – ten years to the day from his first enlistment at Algiers.

With other recruits Dick travelled to Marseilles where they were to catch a boat for Oran. On the way the young man made a detour to see Simone and to explain the reason for his disappearance. Apparently she had been experiencing her own doubts and seemed relieved when he left to join his comrades.

Once that problem was out of the way he travelled from Oran to Sidi-Bel-Abbes with every intention of becoming, '*Un Bon Legionnaire*,' in fact the best Legionnaire in his regiment. Within days he applied to join the Peloton Des Eleves Caporaux, the platoon for the training of corporals. Having completed the training once before, he was determined to obtain promotion as fast as possible. Within a short time he was accepted and after training, he passed out the first of thirty trainees.

On the 18th April 1925 Dick left Sidi-Bel-Abbes with the 21st Company of the 6th Battalion on their way to the Moroccan Riff Mountains. Their destination was Fez, the capital of Morocco, where they were to join a mobile group commanded by Colonel Freydenberg. With two other groups they were to fight on a front of some fifty miles, stretching from Bab-Morouj, north of Taza, to Bibabe north of Fez.

Freydenberg's mobile group comprised: the Legion battalion, two battalions of the Regiment Tirailleurs Senegalais, four of the Regiment Tirailleurs Nord Africain, a company of armoured cars, two batteries of 65mm guns, two batteries of 75mm guns, two 105mm guns and one 155mm gun, plus a few reconnaissance planes and about four hundred partisans. In all there were ten thousand men and each of the other two groups had a similar number, making a force of some thirty thousand.

The 6th Battalion comprised the 21st Company under Captain Villiers de Moriame; the 22nd Company, Captain Peckoff; the 23rd Company, Captain Billou and the 24th Company, Captain Anjou. As they marched out of Sidi-Bel-Abbes, marching before them went the famous band of the Legion playing the regimental march, The Boudin (Black Pudding). After that the men sang a song composed by Legionnaires in the 1914 war. The Legion band was reputedly the best in the French Army, superior to even that of the Garde Republicain.

France had been drawn into the war that Abd-el Krim was waging in the mountains against Spain. Abd-el Krim, or to give him his full name Si Mohammed Ben Abd-el-Krim el Jatabi, was an able general, leading fierce and fearless warriors. He had vowed he would not rest until his homeland had complete independence. The Arabs believed in him. He had gained the support of many tribes by preaching of a Holy War where the tribes would unite and drive out the infidel.

They were heading to an area where impregnable mountain strongholds contrasted with fertile valleys. On their approach, through the eastern section, they saw the towering mountains of Djebel Hamman, Bou Zineb and Azrou Akchar sweeping down towards the town of Taza. Dwarf palms in the foothills gave way to thuya trees, evergreen oaks and cedars at high altitudes. In the valleys flourished olives, vines, barley, figs and oranges. On the southern slopes of the Riff most of the rivers dried up in the summer months, providing a sound surface for men and mules to walk upon. These riverbeds were a godsend to the Legion for there were no roads. The only man made paths had been beaten out by the footsteps of centuries. Danger came when winter storms, which could last for weeks, transformed the riverbeds into dirty yellow torrents.

The men had travelled by train to Oujda, on the Moroccan frontier, and they rested there under canvas. From Oujda they travelled to Taza on a little military train, known as the Taco, set on a sixty-centimetre track. Then there came a forced march to Fez and a rendezvous with the other sections of Freydenberg's outfit.

They left Fez on 30th April with Dick's group heading for the outpost of Ain Aisha, on the Ouergha River – the area dominated by Abd-el Krim. They were to smash their way through to besieged outposts and evacuate some of them. These included Amzez, Ain Leu, Astar, Sker, Bou Azoun, Ain-Djenane, Taounat, Mediouna, Bou Alima and Bab-Taza.

Cut off in rugged country they often felt they were engaged in a private struggle against the tribesmen. It was unlike any military exercise they had ever known. The tribesmen had no headquarters and no lines of communication. They fought on their own initiative, experts at camouflage; they knew how to make best use of the terrain. They always travelled light, carrying only the bare essentials of food, rifles and minimum ammunition. This meant they were superior in mobility compared with the European soldiers who were burdened with standard packs.

The 6th Battalion left Ain Aisha on 5th May and with the River Ouergha on their right, they descended into a valley. The beleaguered fort of Taounat was a couple of miles ahead, sitting on a wooded hilltop above the village. As they advanced, the enemy fired down on them from the slopes. Dick was with the 21st Company in the centre of the wedge-shaped advance, the 22nd were to the right, the 23rd to the left with the 24th held in reserve. No shots were fired by the Legionnaires, who never wasted bullets on obscure targets. Instead, they fixed bayonets and charged into the trees. Seeing they were outnumbered, the Riffs fled from around the fort.

Stealthily, the Legionnaires entered the village seeking out any snipers who might have been left. Suddenly an Arab leapt up from the flat roof of a house and fired, fatally wounding Captain Villiers de Moriame in the chest. The shot was still ringing in their ears as Dick returned the fire, shooting the assailant through the head, watching motionless as the man tumbled into the street.

From then on there was little respite and each day they would march ten to fifteen miles in full kit. There were daily skirmishes as they reinforced or evacuated the outposts. The soldiers would find suitable camp sites, pitch their tents, dig trenches and mount guard. Still the tribesmen would manage to infiltrate their positions, stealing guns and whenever possible murdering the unwelcome intruders to their lands.

The fighting continued for months with moments of despair, heroism, comedy and occasional boredom, stories far too numerous to recount here.

Following a minor injury, Dick had a spell in hospital at Taza. The hospital staff was under constant pressure trying to deal with the wounded, many having suffered horrific injuries. Once again Dick found himself giving a helping hand only to find that a number of the patients were known to him, people he had served with during his career. Captain Billou arrived with two bullet holes in his cheek and his right leg was partially severed above the knee. Dick assisted during the operation on the captain and then went to sit with him for a while on the ward. The injured man opened his eyes and gave Dick a grin...... he winked, smiled again and closing his eyes, he died.

With barely time to reflect on the horror of war, Dick was sent to bring in another patient from the overflowing veranda where the injured waited for attention. Assisted by an orderly he gently lifted a stretcher on which lay a Legionnaire, totally covered by a blanket with his kepi resting upon his chest. The blanket had been used to hide the awful state of the face and body of the man on the stretcher, so terrible were his wounds. Even in a hospital well used to seeing the most appalling injuries someone had felt the need to conceal the soldier from view. As they lowered the man to the operating table Dick gave an anguished cry. There before him lay his friend Schneider.

The two men had lost touch after leaving Colomb Bechar. Schneider's evacuation papers stated that his unit was the Compagnie Monte of Kenadza, so he must have gone back to their faithful mule, Aisha. She was probably waiting for him somewhere in the Riff.

Gone was the man who had been his companion in the desert. Schneider had a bullet in the middle of his spine. He was completely paralysed. Wounded a week previously, he had lain for days in a gully and had been found by sheer luck. By the time they had got him to hospital his body was in a state of putrefaction.

"There is nothing I can do for the poor chap," the surgeon spoke half to himself.

"How long?" Dick whispered.

"He may last a day, an hour, a week. It is in the hands of God."

Schneider was tied into a large body splint and put on to a bed in a side room. Dick sat with him whenever he could, desperate to help his friend while knowing there was nothing that could be done to save him. Eventually Schneider drifted away and his friend could only say thank you to God for taking the man and freeing him from such excruciating pain.

Having returned to active duty, Dick was recommended for promotion to sergeant. While he had been away most of his friends had volunteered for service in Syria and Tonkin (Vietnam). Their replacements were recruits who had just finished their four months initial training. One of these recruits was a drunken Russian who was determined not to conform; he consistently refused to wash and was continually fighting and causing problems among the men. Time and time again he was warned about his behaviour but he was always belligerent in his attitude, eventually throwing down his jacket and gesturing that he wanted to fight the Sergeant. Finally, removing his own jacket, Dick gave the man the long deserved thrashing he had been asking for. Within the Legion this rough and ready justice was usually considered the soft option and preferable to the horrors of the prison regime.

Although the fight had been absolutely fair, the Russian was not going to take any punishment without complaint knowing that the sergeant could be disciplined. Dick was reported by the man and consequently he faced the prospect of a court martial for hitting a subordinate.

Initially he was placed in jail while the general in command considered his case. Then he was handcuffed to eight other accused Legionnaires and sent to the Chateau Neuf, the military prison at Oran. Dick occupied the same cell into which he had been flung with Schneider at the end of their desertion. Their names and the date of their capture were still there, carved on the concrete wall. Under them Dick chiselled his name once again and the date of his latest detention. As an after thought he added the words jamais deux sans trois (never twice without a third).

Dick's trial came at the end of 1926. A court of seven officers was presided over by a colonel. The prosecutor was also an officer. A civilian lawyer defended Dick. First of all an outline of his career was read to the court and then the prosecutor waded into Dick, dwelling on the desertion and the spell in the Penal Battalion. On the other hand his own lawyer brought the unblemished record of his first enlistment and his decorations to the notice of the court, making a brilliant plea for leniency. The officers retired to consider their verdict and Dick was taken to the courtyard, under escort, to await the decision.

When it came, the decision read:-

·*In the name of the French people and the President of the Republic, through the laws which are conferred on the President of the Court-Martial, the detained is acquitted, not guilty.*

Only when he returned to Sidi-Bel-Abbes did Dick discover that, although acquitted, he had been reduced to the ranks. This meant he had to be posted to another battalion, the 9th Company of the 3rd Battalion at Ain Sefra, the headquarters of the Compagnies Sahariennes.

Trains from Oran carried tourists through Ain Sefra to Beni-Ounif, further south, to see the Roman ruins at Le Figuig. The passengers' interest in ruins must have been all consuming for them to even consider travelling in that sweatbox of a train. Tired and limp, the tourists would tumble out of the train and on to the platform at Ain Sefra to stretch their legs in temperatures reaching 108 degrees Fahrenheit. On his days off Dick would go to meet the train and, wearing his best uniform, never failed to attract the British passengers. Not only did he enjoy talking to the visitors but they also brought English newspapers, magazines and books, many of which they would happily spare for his collection.

The personal column of the Times provided him with the address of Toc H in England. This opened a new door for the Legionnaire in the form of a pen friend. Harry McGregor Pearson was the son of the Reverend Harry Pearson who was then the secretary of the London Police Court Mission. The two young men corresponded for years. With the books sent to him by Harry Pearson, Dick filled a number of gaps in his education. Gibbon's The Decline and Fall of the Roman Empire was among the many volumes he read from cover to cover.

One of the attractions of Ain Sefra was its location, north of Colomb Bechar yet still in the desert. Always a man to spend some time alone, Dick would wander off into the dunes where he literally took to hunting mirages. When a mirage appeared he sat down, almost afraid to breathe in case he frightened it away. He saw great phantom towns, with tall shining minarets and beautiful villas set amid oleander and bougainvillea. Trees weighted down with figs and pomegranates. Then there were the lakes, enormous shimmering expanses of blue water. Never once did he see people. The lakes he knew were an optical illusion caused by the heat rising from the desert. But, what of those ghostly cities? Were they figments of his imagination or freak projections of actual places, maybe hundreds of miles away?

Requests for reinforcements reached Ain Sefra from the three regiments stationed in Morocco. Individuals had no choice and went, without question, to anywhere they were drafted. Dick was selected with nineteen others for the 4th Regiment at Marrakech. Catching the train at 9am they travelled north, first to Macheria and then to Le Kreider where the Legion had a barracks and a huge farm. The rickety wooden railed train rattled on into Morocco by way of Oujda and then westwards to Taza, Fez, Meknes and Casablanca finally south to Marrakech.

Soon after arrival the men were paraded for inspection by Colonel Mathieu, who remembered Dick from the Riff campaign. He questioned the young man. "How would you like to go into a company where you can speak English?"

"Very much," the reply came promptly. Dick seldom had the chance to practice his mother tongue.

The battalion was building roads under the command of Major De Corta, a great character who was known and liked throughout the Legion. The Company Dick was to join was at Tines Gadaouine and the following morning he hitched a lift on the supply lorry. The driver left the Marrakech to Mogador road at Chichaoua, going south towards Imintanout. The scenery was breathtaking but its wild beauty concealed the ugly presence of poverty and death that overshadowed the lives of the inhabitants. For three years there had been a drought with the resulting crop failures and starvation of man and beast.

Leaving Imintanout they found themselves in desolate farming areas. It was here they saw children, little more than six years old, huddling together for warmth. A little further on the Legionnaires came across a family who were mourning the loss of two children who had died only a few hours before. They came to a village where mothers offered their daughters for sale, intending to use the money to feed the younger children and keep themselves alive. The two men gave the villagers their own supplies but it was impossible for them to stay and do more.

As they were nearing their destination, Dick and the driver stopped to pass the time of day with some mountain tribesmen known as Chleuhs. They sat together on a large flat-topped rock discussing the progress being made in the country when Dick heard the familiar cry, "toubib!" More men were joining them from the mountain path and they were being led by a tall, good-looking, Arab. "Salaam, toubib," the man said again.

"Toubib? You know me?" Questioned Dick.

Apparently the young man was one of the nomads from the plain of Tamlelt and they had met four years earlier. It was very likely the bush telegraph would once again go into action telling the local people that Dick was a healer.

Eventually they arrived at Tines Gadaouine and Dick discovered the source of the English conversation promised by Colonel Mathieu. The company commander was Prince Djintcharadze, one of a number of Georgian princes who joined the Legion after the Russian Revolution. Lieutenant Djintcharadze could speak English fluently and the two men became good friends. Many years later they were destined to meet again in very different surroundings.

11 Kingly

The 9th Company in the 3rd Battalion of the 4th Regiment was short of mules. This offered an excellent chance for selected volunteers to travel to the market at Marrakech. Legionnaire Cooper, the most experienced in the Regiment, was at the front of the queue when he heard of the forthcoming outing. On the strength of his spell with Aisha in the Compagnie Montee, he managed to convince Lieutenant Djintcharadze that he was an expert muleteer. A couple of hours later, four men and a sergeant set off for the 10th Company base where transport would be made available for their trip to town.

On the outskirts of the 10th base, the men saw a group of Arabs and Jews carrying chickens and eggs to barter with the Legion cooks. As they approached, a man called out "Salaam, toubib." The call was taken up by others and a young lad rushed towards them holding out his hand to Dick. The boy had a nasty gash running the length of his forearm and Dick guided him to the company first aid station. The Legionnaire in charge, having heard the Arabs calling to Dick, automatically assumed that he must be a doctor, and so he provided all that was needed to disinfect and dress the youngster's wound.

As the party had been delayed by the casualty it was late in the evening when the lorries finally pulled into Marrakech, an ideal time to sample the local delights but too late to shop for mules. Much later that night the men stretched out in the back of the canvas covered vehicles, grabbing a couple of hours sleep before the market opened.

In the morning, half asleep, the men wandered towards a double compound where a large number of mules were tethered. The compound was separated into two parts by barbed wire. One section contained the able, working mules and in the other section was a motley group of animals, most of whom had seen better days. The best they could hope for was to be chosen by a European as a pet.

Studying the mules in the first section, the soldiers made their selection and completed the bargaining with the owners. They arranged for the animals to be issued with numbers, to be branded on their rear hooves once back at the camp and then led them to water. As they passed the other section of the compound there was an almighty disturbance which attracted everyone's attention. Mules were kicking and biting at each other and above that noise a shrill, almost human, cry could be heard. Turning casually to lean over the rickety barrier, Dick saw the reason for the hullabaloo and couldn't believe his eyes. He took a second look and this time yelled at the top of his voice, "Aisha!".

The mule had scented him and was fighting the rope that held her to a wooden post. Dick leapt the railing and threw his arms round her neck, letting her nuzzle in his ear. As he held her, Aisha made sounds as if to tell him all that had happened to her since they had parted so suddenly at Kenadza. His pleasure at finding the mule was tempered by the knowledge that she was to be auctioned the following day. That night the Legionnaires watched as Dick wandered over to the compound and let the mule snuggle into his shoulder for they could understand the bonds between man and beast.

Obviously they had to work out a plan and save the mule for their comrade. Calling Dick over they went into a huddle to discuss the details. Putting the plan into operation proved a lot easier than they had thought. The sergeant organised a whip round to buy as much wine as possible, then a couple of them sauntered to the mule compound to keep the guard company. The three of them were drinking well into the night until eventually they all collapsed in a heap under the water trough. This was the moment Dick had been waiting for. He glided quietly passed the snoring group to untether Aisha from the rail. The mule started to make a noise as he approached and it took all his persuading to quieten her down as he led her away to safety.

Aisha was hidden in an old building on the edge of the town. It was reasonably easy to collect her the next morning as they were returning to camp in convoy. System D had been put into use in true Legionnaire fashion.

It was also fairly simple to smuggle Aisha back to camp but once there, Lieutenant Djintcharadze was not so easily fooled. "We appear to have one animal too many," he said, stating the obvious. "Do you men have a problem with simple arithmetic?"

As luck would have it, the Lieutenant was a natural horseman. Having been raised in the Caucasus he was unlikely to cause any problems about Aisha. Dick requested a private chat with him and they walked together towards the officer's tent. The soldier had to admit to his activities in purloining the mule for although they had all been involved in the deception, the other men had only done so to help him out. Djin, as the men had come to call the officer, listened sympathetically and, as the explanation came to a close, said that he hadn't a clue what Cooper was talking about and would he please go away and get on with some work.

Once again Dick became a muleteer, caring for Aisha and another mule he decided to call Scratch. Proving herself to be particularly sure-footed, Aisha was promoted to 'carrier of the officer's drinks chest.'

Orders arrived instructing the Battalion to transfer to Dar Lahoussine, the furthermost outpost in southern Morocco, an area where the tribesmen were still resisting French rule. Beyond this were the River Dra and Mauritania. They camped on the land of the Ida Ou Zal tribe in the High Atlas before starting the march down to the fertile Sous Plain en route to Agadir. The men pitched their tents on a plateau and the rest of the day they were free of duties. Many of the soldiers took to their tents to sleep or read, while others decided to wash their clothes in the cool tingling waters of a spring. Dick wandered up the mountain slopes, searching for wild asparagus beneath the clinging bushes.

Enjoying the solitude and the fresh mountain air, Dick sat for a while on a huge cream coloured boulder contemplating his future. Inevitably, his thoughts turned to the past. It was at moments like this that he felt close to Lucy and at peace with the world. In his mind he could hear her singing their favourite lullaby and he could hear the voices of his brother and sister as they begged for a story, before settling down to sleep. Other sounds penetrated his day dreams. He could hear a dog whining and his thoughts turned to Osman and the day he took him to Garcia.

Again he could hear the whining. This time it sounded like a number of young animals complaining. Realising the sounds were real and not just in his head, he stood up and listened more carefully, trying to trace the source of the noise. Deciding the cries were coming from above, he made his way further up the mountain side. Jackals could be the answer! Maybe they had been abandoned! With this thought he had left himself with no alternative but to investigate. He could not leave pups to die – be they jackals or otherwise.

His curiosity aroused, he looked around, stopping occasionally to listen again. Eventually he found the mouth of a deep cave and lighting a match, he edged inside, wary of a possible attack. Peering into the distance he could see four young jackals lying on a bed of dried leaves and twigs. They looked about a month old. There was a fifth animal snuggled in the middle of them, a creamy ball with flapping ears and it was not in the least bit frightened of him.

Dick took another look around. These animals seemed reasonably healthy and that meant they had parents nearby. Parents who would be very angry at his intrusion and who might well decide to oust him forcibly, or worse. The creamy ball waddled towards him on stumpy legs and Dick could see it was a dog puppy. It was likely that its mother had died in the recent drought and the jackals – who had possibly gone to eat some flesh – had adopted her offspring.

Delighted with his find, Dick scooped up the little ball of fur and got out of the cave as quickly as possible. All the way down the mountain the pup snuggled against him and Dick christened him Osmaniki, 'Osman' in memory of his first pet and 'Iki' being the Turkish word for two.

Nearly everyone at the camp made a fuss of the new recruit and before long they had shortened his name to Iki. Legionnaires brought milk for the pup and the first aider supplied a rubber glove to act as a teat. The animal was adopted as the company's official pet and was entered as such for ration purposes. Next on the agenda was a boisterous introduction to Aisha as the puppy danced around her hooves yapping noisily. The mule was obviously pleased with their new little friend.

A bed was made for Iki inside the officer's drinks chest. There was very little milk to be had on the camp and the few tins they did have were reserved for the officer's rice pudding

– a luxury for Sunday lunch. Members of the company tried to beg or borrow milk for the pup with little success. The cooks were adamant that they could not have the tinned milk. Even bribery failed, so they reverted to the unfailing method of System D and stole every tin.

As a consequence, rice pudding was taken off the menu. No doubt the officers guessed the reason why, but they were unlikely to complain. Who would believe them? Legionnaires didn't steal milk! A barrel of wine, perhaps! But milk, never!

With his diet assured, Iki thrived. Indeed, the puppy was so popular with his masters that they began to spoil him with kindness. After some discussion and not a little argument, everyone agreed that Dick should train and care for the animal.

Reaching Agadir, the Legionnaires marched on between the High Atlas and the Anti Atlas Mountains, inhabited by the great Chiouka tribe. The battalion took up the fighting formation as they drew closer to the Anti Atlas Mountains, where most of the tribes were not pacified. Here, tribal groups were not simply up in arms against the French but also permanently at war with each other. They passed the Biougra outpost without mishap and two days later the 9th Company took possession of Dar Lahoussine ou Aomar, which had formerly housed the Caid of the Ait Ouguidern tribe, before he declared war on the French. Within two days, the rest of the battalion returned to Agadir, leaving the 9th Company to control the area.

Dar Lahoussine stood on high ground strewn with knee high boulders. It was a large, strongly-built dwelling surrounded by four tall walls, each about two hundred yards long. In the centre, like the keep of an English castle, was a thirty-foot high watchtower topped by a flagstaff from which the tricolour hung in limp folds. Legionnaires completed the defences by building machine gun posts on the walls. Some distance out from the walls were coils of barbed wire, laid not only to discourage warring tribesmen but also to prevent hyenas and jackals causing false alarms at night.

The biggest obstacle to comfortable living at the fortress was the lack of water. Each morning it was necessary to take the mules, loaded with barrels, to collect spring water from a distance of some three miles or more. Their dependence on so distant a water supply left them all particularly vulnerable to attack. A few weeks after they had arrived, one of the soldiers, Legionnaire Damone Collini, started to walk around the camp pretending to be water divining, with a forked stick. Everyone laughed at him and he was continually being teased that he was really looking for wine, until the day arrived when the stick began to twitch rapidly. Now they all paid serious attention, taking turns to dig on the spot trying to find water inside the fort. After some pretty hard toil, the ground at the bottom of the hole started to look dark as water began to bubble its way to the surface. Up went a shout and the Legionnaires were congratulating each other, shaking hands and patting each other on the back. They seemed to have forgotten their previous scepticism and who had started the search and then had the patience to continue looking for the water regardless of their jibes. The whole activity had been watched over by the newly arrived, Corsican officer, Lieutenant Vecchioni, who heartily congratulated Legionnaire Collini's initiative.

Life settled down in the camp with regular patrols and occasional perilous skirmishes. Dick spent all of his spare time with the mule and the pup. How people could associate mules with stupidity or stubbornness was beyond the young man. Aisha was intelligent, affectionate, willing to learn and, by common consent, the cleverest mule in the French Foreign Legion. If she were allowed to run free during a march, the mule would trot along the file of soldiers looking for one with an open haversack carrying food, usually bread, inside.

She would then lick the back of the man's neck, tip his kepi forward on to the ground and grab his bread as he bent to retrieve his hat. Occasionally she would trot beside the men suddenly sticking out her foreleg, tripping them up as they marched. With haversacks splayed open on the ground, Aisha would be selective, picking up chocolate or, on occasions, gripping a tin of sardines in her teeth. Then she would trot back to Dick for him to open it.

Iki was by now fully grown and could run like the wind. Every morning dog and master would exercise together. At first they kept close to the walls within the protective cover of the machine guns. Gradually they gained confidence and strayed further and further from the camp. Iki would streak away disappearing among the rocks until a whistle would bring him bounding back to Dick, the same sounding whistle that had called Osman to heel many years before.

One morning they took a new direction, heading south, and after a few hundred yards they came to a steep footpath leading up to a rocky promontory. The dog chased ahead up the path, sometimes stopping to explore a new smell with his nose wrinkled and, at other times, snapping at the tails of dancing insects. Eventually the animal clambered on a ledge and disappeared from sight. Dick reached the spot and could hear Iki barking, then whimpering and at times growling. Hauling himself up on the ledge, Dick stopped dead, before him was a large rock shelf and on the shelf, an eagle.

The mighty bird, with a wing span of some six feet, appeared to be injured and was hopping about in a feeble attempt to seek refuge from the inquisitive dog. Crying in pain and desperation the eagle flapped one huge but ineffectual wing at the interloper. As Dick tore a strip from his shirt the bird lashed out at him with his beak in a brave show of defiance. With a great deal of patience, the Legionnaire finally managed to grab the bird and tie its beak. As he did so he could see a large gash on its wing, close to its breast. Furthermore, the bird had quite obviously broken its leg.

Holding the eagle firmly between his legs, Dick improvised a pencil splint for the broken leg. Then, tucking the huge bird under his arm and holding its head with his free hand, Dick set off back to the camp – sending Iki racing on ahead to get help.

When the dog arrived back at the camp without his master the Legionnaires immediately organised a search party. To their relief the lookout shouted the news that their comrade was coming in. "He's carrying something heavy," the man added. Two or three of the men raced towards Dick to give him a hand but he warned them off, anxious not to frighten the bird any more than necessary.

They took the injured eagle into the stables and leaving his beak tied, Dick set about bathing and disinfecting the injuries and replacing the splint. A suitable ring and chain were found and, after some adjustment, were attached to the bird's leg and he was tethered to one of the roof supports. Finally they removed the tie from his beak. The bird made no attempt to struggle and perched on a beam looking back at his captors as though he knew they were trying to help him.

Leaving the eagle to rest on a bed of straw, the men held a conference to decide what food to offer him. "Rats," was the favoured suggestion. "Rabbits," said another. Finally they organised a foraging party to search for anything which may be the eagle's natural prey. Meanwhile the bird settled down to sleep but each time Iki ventured too close he would hiss at the animal with his feathers raised in warning.

One by one the foragers returned with a weird assortment of fauna. One had been particularly enterprising and showed his friends a jar containing five lizards. Another had a snake; there were one or two moles and a couple of smaller rodents. The cook arrived with some chunks of meat that the others viewed with suspicion, convinced – and rightly so – that it was their dinner. Everything was spread out before the bird and Legionnaires were vying for position to see which delicacy he would prefer. The moles turned out to be his favourite food.

Lieutenant Vecchioni complained bitterly about Dick's zoo! Not content with an extra mule, he had brought back a dog and now Aquila. The officer had used the bird's true Latin name and from then on it was known around the camp as Aquila.

By trial and error they discovered that the eagle could go for several days without food and they were careful not to overfeed it. Iki had managed to gain a lot of ground with the bird and eventually reached the point where they became firm friends. It was wonderful to see Aquila sitting patiently on the straw bed with Iki's head beneath its wing. Aisha would watch their every move, more than a little jealous of the new resident in the stable.

Things had been so quiet around the camp that they had almost forgotten the reason they were there and that the hostile tribes still posed a serious threat. A night attack by fifty or so tribesmen took them completely unawares and two of the guards on the watchtower were slightly injured. The attackers were soon routed, leaving about ten of their dead outside the sturdy walls of the outpost.

Once again peace and quiet befell the camp and eight weeks after his arrival, the men decided it was time to release the powerful bird back to the wild. No one could bear to see the noble creature imprisoned in a stable now he was well. The chain was removed from his foot and Aquila was taken into the yard. For a moment he blinked in the sunlight, unsure of what to do. Suddenly he flexed and flapped his wings, sending his audience running for cover. His wing span now seemed far greater than they first thought. A few more flaps of his wings and Aquila was off, soaring above them to some three or four hundred feet. After circling a few times the bird swooped down, landing on the central watchtower where he stayed for the next half an hour.

Throughout the event, Iki raced up and down the yard barking encouragement to his friend. Occasionally he would stop in his tracks and then leap up and down on his hind legs throwing his head back and almost somersaulting in his efforts to see the bird. It was the sight of food that finally tempted Aquila from its high perch and he glided down to the stable entrance close to his bed.

The eagle became incredibly tame, staying close to the camp. When the mules were taken for exercise, Aquila would follow high above. By this time, the members of Dick's menagerie were all close friends. On one occasion, spiralling high above the mules, Aquila almost disappeared from sight and then suddenly, from being the merest speck in the sky, plummeted down onto Aisha's back. The mule leapt in pain as the talons dug into her bare hide. From then on, Aisha wore a saddle when she was out and Aquila dive-bombed her on a regular basis without causing further injury.

One of the most amazing things to watch was Aquila playing with sheep. When Dick first spotted her flapping in the middle of the flock he panicked, running towards her to chase her away from the lambs. Then he realised that far from attacking the lambs, the bird was playing with them. They seemed to be playing a game of tag and not one of them ever received so much as a scratch from the huge bird. It was the sight of Aquila with the lambs that prompted Dick to borrow a camera and he managed to capture a unique photograph of them. He also took the opportunity to photograph Aisha and Iki.

Over a period of time Legionnaire Cooper had photo-graphed many events in the history of the French Foreign Legion forming a unique collection.

With the area still quiet, Dick and Iki resumed their walks but now they were joined by Aquila, who would follow them at a great height. If Dick called the bird's name he would level off and skim the ground close by. This was how they were proceeding one afternoon when they came across a young boy, of about seven years of age, who was crying bitterly. The child was terrified when he saw the stranger who could control an eagle. Dick spoke to him in Arabic, asking the reason for his tears. Without speaking, the boy held up his hand to reveal a poisoned wound that had swollen to twice its size. Sitting the boy on a rock and speaking quietly all the time, Dick sterilised his penknife over the flames of matches while the child looked on in fascination. The soldier made an incision into the child's wound releasing the bulge of pus and easing out much of the remainder. He cleaned and dressed the wound with one of the issue dressings he now carried with him as a matter of course.

Several days later, Dick met the young boy at exactly the same place only this time an old man accompanied the child. The man stood beckoning to Dick who moved slowly forward with his hand closed around the butt of his revolver, unsure if he was walking into a trap. To his embarrassment, the old man went down on his knees, praising Allah for sending the doctor to heal the boy. During this performance, Dick noticed that the child's wound was healing well.

The old man was insistent that the Legionnaire should accompany them back to their camp. It was an odd situation. The tribe was at war with the Legion but Dick had no concerns as to his own safety for the old man was genuinely grateful and would repay the healer with nothing but courtesy.

They spent several hours together in the village. Dick sat cross-legged with a group of elders while younger groups approached them with a variety of foods, including couscous with baked sheep's head. For sometime the young man enjoyed the hospitality of his new-found friends, relaxing as they discussed the politics of the region in a friendly fashion.

That evening, Dick sought out the first aider at Dar Lahoussine and in exchange for his ration of wine, managed to obtain a good supply of argyrol, quinine, aspirin and bandages.

A few days later his 'free day' was spent in the tribal village, where he was welcomed as an old and trusted friend. On this occasion he went round the village gathering up all those suffering from bad eyes which he treated with the drops of argyrol. Doing the best he could with his limited knowledge he treated one or two villagers who were obviously suffering from malaria with quinine and then finally he bathed a variety of wounds, bandaging the more serious cases.

Before long the 'healer' received an invitation from a village some ten miles distant. Such was the request that a horse was provided to enable him to travel the distance more quickly. Again he was treated as a king and had to spend some time exchanging pleasantries with the elders, before settling down to 'morning surgery'. On this occasion, sick people from surrounding villages were gathered close to the chieftain's mud-built house. There were about twenty in all, men, women and children, most of them with suppurating eyes. The toubib washed out inflamed eyes with cooled boiled water and applied a weak solution of permanganate of potash as a disinfectant. The prescriptions he relied upon the most were a bath and the cleansing of sores. All the time he was trying to teach as well as to heal.

Malaria was, of course, the most prevalent of the illnesses. Anopheles mosquitoes abounded on the marshy plains and were far from unknown in the mountainous regions. There was little to be done for the one or two who were suffering from anthrax, no doubt contracted from the skin, fur or bones of an infected animal. Smallpox was also allowed to run its course unchecked. A great many of these people carried the calling cards of smallpox, some of them blinded by corneal ulcers. Cases of tuberculosis were evident, picked up from infected milk. A form of leprosy, known in Morocco as jadam, attacked those of Arab stock, yet left unscathed the Jews who lived in the same communities. This paradox made sense when one remembered that the Jews had already adopted Western ideas of hygiene.

A universal affliction of the tribes was scabies, and Dick found numerous cases of 'the itch' in the villages, using sulphur ointment to ease discomfort.

On his clandestine excursions to various tribes, Dick was always accompanied by his dog. One day, young Iki found himself a comely friend. Dick was treating an elderly, wizened, old man when he felt Iki's tail hitting his leg. Each time he told the dog to go away, the tail banged him again until Dick had no choice but to look up from his ministering. Standing behind Iki was a handsome animal, spotted like a Dalmatian, with its tail wagging furiously. Obviously Iki had brought his friend along for his master's approval. Leaving his patient for a few minutes, Dick made a fuss of Iki and then called to the other dog, encouraging it to come to him. Eventually the two made friends while Iki danced around them both in an expression of happiness giving a series of short, sharp, excited barks.

A few days after this event, Iki went missing. Dick wandered out of the camp each day, heading in different directions and whistling for his pet to no avail. Then, as suddenly as he left, Iki was back. This time he was not alone. Apparently he had gone off to court his girlfriend and now he returned home with his bride.

"We cannot house every animal in the area at this outpost!" ranted Lieutenant Vecchioni. "You must get rid of her." Everyone agreed with the sentiments expressed by the officer while having no intentions of carrying out the order, if indeed it was an order. More straw was laid in the corner of the stable and they named the newcomer Katoushka. Both Aisha and Aquila inspected the bitch from a distance and seemed to approve of her joining the menagerie.

It was around this time that Major de Corta, the battalion commander, promoted Dick to Sergeant. His new duties were varied and interesting and included regular trips to Biougra, about twenty miles north, for stores to replenish the outpost. A convoy of Legionnaires and mules would head out under the command of the sergeant and with a heavily armed escort to protect both men and supplies.

Over confidence was always the Legion's great weakness and before long the armed escort had been ordered to other duties. Although the remaining Legionnaires had rifles, they invariably had them on the sling while they led the mules. The journeys had been going on for a few months without any attacks and the very fact that the commander had seen fit to remove the escort, gave the men a false sense of security. Dick's constant warnings went unheeded and he took to leading the group so he could also act as look-out. To the rear he always posted an experienced soldier.

The inevitable happened when thick fog enveloped the convoy of twenty mules and Legionnaires as they returned from a trip. As usual, Dick was leading with his hand rested lightly on Aisha's bridle. Aquila rocked on top of the swaying load which was secured with ropes on to the mule's back. Iki and Katoushka were trotting happily behind. The party was on the home stretch to Dar Lahoussine and most of them were already thinking about dinner when, without warning, a band of tribesmen swept out of the fog attacking with guns and knives. There were about a hundred of the barefooted aggressors who appeared to rise out of the ground itself. So fast was the attack that there was no time to shout an order.

171

Those who were not killed instantly flung themselves onto their stomachs, hoping for the best. As Dick yanked his gun from his holster he was spinning round trying to assess the situation but the fog made it impossible. They were in danger of killing each other if they fired at the shadows. Murky figures were flitting here and there. The occasional shot was heard and also several groans as knives were thrust into flesh.

Aquila had flown away and the two dogs had taken to their heels, hopefully heading home. In the chaos it was faithful Aisha who remained steady as a rock and Dick dropped to her side feigning death. There was nothing to be achieved, except his real demise, if he decided on heroics. Aisha protected him like an iron-shod guard dog. A tribesman, who bent to steal Dick's boots, received a kick in the head from the mule's hind-legs sending him tumbling backwards. Others who came too near were given the same treatment. At last all the mules had been led away by the raiders with the exception of Aisha who defied all attempts to take her. The mule was still battling valiantly as they emptied their guns into her.

Aisha fell onto Dick's back, nearly suffocating him, but in her death throes she saved him from certain death. First she had distracted their assailants and then, by shielding him with her body, they failed to see him as they made a hurried search for survivors.

As the sounds of the tribesmen faded in the distance, Dick had to find the strength to move Aisha and crawl from under her body. He couldn't bear to look at his very faithful friend. It was his duty to check on his men and quickly he made a thorough search of the area. Four Legionnaires were alive and only one of them was wounded. The sergeant left them to make a further search while he retraced his steps to tend to his mule.

For a minute he stood over her without seeing, then, with tears running down his face, he looked directly at her to find her body was moving. There was the slightest movement of her chest. She was breathing! Dropping to his knees, Dick went to lay his ear against her chest and, in doing so, saw the gaping holes in her stomach where the bullets had ripped as they had been fired at point blank range. Her eyes opened as though to question why, why should anyone wish to shoot her? Dick gently stroked her head and tried to avoid her seeing the revolver as he levelled it at her temple. They had known and loved each other for a long time. Dick squeezed the trigger and put his beloved mule out of her misery.

The fog was beginning to lift as Dick organised the survivors, making sure they had searched for any weapons or valuables missed by the tribesmen. They had to make it to Dar Lahoussine and report before they could go back for the bodies of their comrades. They had been marching for half an hour when Iki and Katoushka came pelting towards them with half the company at full gallop behind. Apparently, Aquila had been the first to arrive at the camp, repeatedly zooming down over the heads of the guards and then flying north for a few hundred yards. It was obvious something was wrong and the men were just reporting her behaviour when Iki and Katoushka raced through the gates. The dogs, repeated the actions of the bird, running to the men and then running back out of the camp in the same direction from which they had just arrived.

The survivors returned to Dar Lahoussine with the rescue party to collect mules and side stretchers on which to carry their fallen comrades. Dick tied up the dogs and chained Aquila to stop them following. He wanted to spare them the sight of Aisha lying dead. She had been their friend too.

12 Liberty

Before very long Katoushka had presented Iki with three puppies, but sadly two of them died in infancy. The surviving pup was the image of Iki at the time Dick had found him with the jackals, a bundle of creamy fur. Always on the move with their master, something had to be arranged for the little one to travel with them. The problem was solved quickly and simply when Dick tied a knot in a large table napkin and placed the puppy inside. Within seconds, Iki had gripped the knot between his teeth and from then onwards he carried his offspring everywhere in the sling.

The Legion was the 'fire brigade' of North Africa. Whenever trouble threatened to set a district ablaze, the Legionnaire was called in to damp down the inflamed feelings. So it was that the 3rd Battalion was ordered to central Morocco where an uprising was said to be imminent. The outpost had to be manned in their absence and this job was to be taken over by the 1st Spahis.

It would be impossible to take Aquila with the battalion and out of his natural environment. Although the bird had always insisted on staying with them, essentially he was always free. The only answer was to keep the eagle in the stable until the battalion was well clear of the area. When Dick went to the stable to say his goodbyes, he was sure Aquila knew they were leaving. The man had always known this day would arrive but that knowledge did not make the parting any easier to bear. He made arrangements with the Spahis, telling them when to set Aquila free and begging them to care for her should she ever be in need.

The 1st Spahis presented arms as the battalion marched away followed by Katoushka and Iki, the later carrying his precious bundle. They were to make their way to Agadir via Biougra. As they passed the site where the recent ambush had occurred, the men fell silent. The whole battalion paraded through Agadir before they boarded a ship for Casablanca. Railway trucks which met them on the quayside at Casablanca transported them inland to Berrechid and on to Boujad. From this point they marched, in fighting formation, into the Middle Atlas mountain range as far as Khenifra. Abd-el Krim had surrendered three years earlier but there were still many fanatical tribesmen prepared to die for the cause.

Battalion orders were to patrol an area of two hundred square miles of tribal territory. Each company was given an area of fifty square miles and instructed to patrol in circles. This strategy was being used more and more throughout the region. The tribesmen found it difficult to recognise one European from another and it became almost impossible when they were all wearing the same uniform and kepis. By covering the area in circles, they gave the impression of being a new company every time they passed, and this way the battalion appeared to be ten times its actual strength of a thousand men.

Dick was with the 9th Company and the sector allotted to them was from Khenifra to Sidi-Lamine, south to Takebald and then over the Bou Haddou Height and back to Khenifra. At night time Iki, Katoushka and the pup, which had now been christened Azer, would take over the watch. They could scent a tribesman miles away and quickly raise the alarm if prowlers were about.

During leisure periods, the men preferred to camp near the Oum er Rebia, the second longest river in Morocco. These waters tumbled down from the Middle Atlas Mountains, flowing west into the Atlantic at Azemmour, north of Masagan. The Legionnaires would bathe and wash their clothes in the river that reached Khenifra through a deep, narrow valley.

Dick had to keep a close watch on the dogs during these breaks as occasionally a bored soldier would take to teasing one or the other of them. Whenever possible he would take them off on their own where he could, groom them, play with them and occasionally, teach them some tricks. One Sunday afternoon, Dick grabbed a couple of towels and set off along the river bank with the three dogs. Iki and Katoushka stayed fairly close, sometimes stopping briefly to identify a new smell. Azer bounced ahead of them all, at times racing off after an imaginary friend and at other times barking incessantly at an illusive foe.

The river was fast running and so Dick chose a stretch where an almond-shaped island afforded a resting place mid-stream. Tossing the towels on to the ground he jumped into the water which, at a guess, was between seven and eight feet deep and he swam across to the island. Iki and Katoushka jumped into the water after him but Azer was unsure of himself, sitting on the bank wagging his tail madly in excitement. The two dogs were making good progress until they reached about halfway when the current began to take them downstream. Seeing they were struggling, Dick dived in to help but they were taken further away from him by the strong current. Azer, aware that something was wrong, was chasing along the bank after his parents, barking and whimpering as he went.

They were fast approaching the tip of the island, the point where the divided arms of the river were reunited in a vicious whirlpool. Iki had his head held high with his front paws pounding at the water while Katoushka was obviously tiring, being pulled down until her nose barely cleared the rushing water. There was approximately ten yards between Dick and the two dogs when the animals disappeared. Dick dived in an effort to save them but he was gripped by the swirling water, sandwiched between two smooth walls. The current from one stream prevented him from rising to the surface while the other stopped him from going deeper. It was then he saw the dogs gyrating with him, close to him, like feathers spinning in a whirlwind. Lunging forward with both hands outstretched, Dick grabbed both dogs by their necks and clutched them to him.

He knew they were all close to death and as snapshot images of his life began to flash before him he heard a familiar voice. "Let go of the dogs." It was Lucy speaking. "Let go of the dogs," the voice commanded him. Again, for the third time she spoke. "Let go of the dogs and give yourself to the water." Dick obeyed.

Some miracle brought his limp body to the surface; no doubt science would have an answer. However, there was no explanation for the voice he had heard and the instructions he had obeyed against all the instincts of self-preservation.

Exhausted, he clung on to a clump of dried reeds. Coughing and spluttering he tried desperately to get his breath. A noise droned though his head. On and on it went until he eventually realised that it was Azer, whimpering softly somewhere above him. Forcing himself to take control, Dick managed to get onto the riverbank where he collapsed face down. The young dog wriggled along the ground on his stomach - pushing himself close into his master's side and, a couple of hours later, that's exactly where a patrol of Legionnaires found them.

A couple of the soldiers stayed with Dick while the others continued further down-river until they came across the bodies of Iki and Katoushka. Once the animals had ceased their struggles against death, the water had carried them away to toss them to the surface hundreds of yards downstream. The men buried the two dogs in the spot where the river had finally given them up.

In the days that followed it was a subdued man that sat with his dog gazing out across the river. Dick had little to say to anyone, constantly turning questions over in his mind that appeared to have no answers. He was not surprised when a few days later he was summoned to the tent of his commanding officer and given more disturbing news.

Lieutenants Djintcharadze and Vecchioni were seated behind tables in the makeshift accommodation when Dick arrived and gave the customary salute. He could tell from their expressions that the news was going to be bad. The mail had just arrived from Marrakech and in it was a communication from the British Consulate in Messina telling Dick that his father had died on 13th October 1929.

Two months later Dick was still seeking answers to his questions when he decided the time had come to leave the Legion Etranger and see what civilian life had to offer. His five year tour of duty was at an end and so by the time Christmas arrived he had made all his arrangements, including finding a good home for Azer. They would miss each other terribly but it was impossible for Dick to take the dog with him for he had no idea of what lay ahead.

A summary of the French Foreign Legion career of Dick Cooper, including the battles in which he participated is entered in his Military Book:

Dardanelles, 1st March 1915 to 4th September 1915, Sahara, 10th October 1919 to 10th October 1920, Algeria,

War in Morocco and Central Sahara from 1920 to 1925.

The very busy year of 1925 included seven battles in May alone:-

Taounat, 4th May: Bab-Ouender, 6th May: Salsafa, 8th May: Gara-Meziat, 14th May: Ain-Djenane, 23rd May: The capture of Astar outpost, 4th June: the battles of Ain-Matouf, 6th June and Mediouna 7th June: the battles of the River Amar, 13th June: Dar Caid-Bachir, 14th July and River Amelil, 18th July: the capture of Bibane outpost, 20th August: the battle of Djebel Nador and other battles in the area, Bab-Moroudj outpost, Kiffane and Camp Roches, 2nd September.

A separate entry marks the co-operation with Franco-Spanish troops and his service in South Algeria 1926 to 1927.

The final item records the fact that he took part in the pacification of the South Moroccan Territories: Dar Caid Lahoussine ou Aomar, Beni Mallal, Asilal and Imintanout.

The dates given are those on which orders were received for specific engagements.

The medals awarded to Dick included:

Croix de Guerre, by two.

Medaille Commemorative de la Grande Guerre.

Medaille Commemorative d'Orient.

Medaille d'Engagement Volontaire.

Medaille Coloniale.

Medaille de la Paix de Maroc.

French Victory Medal

British Victory Medal

British General Service Medal.

So ended eleven and a half years of service with the French Foreign Legion, years in which he had experienced heaven and hell. The Legion had been his friend, a parent, his torturer, and it had given him a home.

Dick left Marrakech on the Casablanca train. From Casablanca he took the boat to Marseilles where he met his sister Daisy, who was at that time living in Nice. It was less than twenty-four hours since the Legion door had closed behind him and already he felt lost. In particular it was the women who were a closed book to him. With the exception of a brief period between enlistments, he had been in North Africa for ten years and most of the women there were of Arab origin and untainted by the vices of the Western world.

Having booked rooms in a local hotel for a few nights, Dick left his sister to rest while he renewed his acquaintance with Marseilles. It was the evening of 8th January 1930 and he walked up and down the Canebiere, savouring the new experience of being a civilian again. Eventually he entered the Café Riche, ordered a drink and sat gazing around the big room absorbing every detail. He had a feeling of being watched but decided he was just being fanciful. Then he felt it again and this time looked more closely at the individual faces of people scattered around the room. For a few moments his glance rested on a delightful group of a mother with her children. The woman was elegantly dressed and her three little girls were as pretty as a picture. As Dick continued to study the group he realised there was something familiar about the woman. Who was she?

For a few moments he looked away and then, like a magnet, his eyes were drawn again to her direction. This time he caught her staring back at him and simultaneously they recognised each other. Fifteen years had passed since he had romped with the countess's niece in the hotspots of Marseilles. They smiled nervously at each other across the room and then Dick plucked up the courage to walk over to her table. For a while they chatted, recalling the old days, catching up with more recent news. He discovered that soon after he had left her, Stephanie had married a banker. The three little girls were hers and they all lived happily in a lovely villa at La Valentine. Eventually they parted as friends who knew they would never meet again.

After a few more days Dick said his farewells to his sister and set off by train for Paris. For a very long time he had promised himself a night at the Paris Opera and he looked forward to it as a child looks forward to Christmas.

Walking along the Boulevard des Italiens, Dick was accosted by a prostitute. Looking beyond the heavy make-up and the emptiness in her eyes, he saw before him a petite young girl who could accompany him to the opera. Instead of going to her room he took her to see Tosca. That evening in Paris, the prostitute became a princess because that was what he wanted her to be. They held hands as Cavaradossi sat on the rampart to write a last letter before facing the firing squad, recalling how the stars shone on him and Tosca when they met. The pathos of E Lucevan le Stelle sent tears trickling down Dick's face.

When he had left the Legion he had thought that nothing could touch him. He had witnessed so much killing, sickness, poverty, depravation and sadness. He had met with cheats, liars, thieves, thugs and murderers. Thankfully there had been times when he had seen the other side of life and for that he would be eternally grateful. That he still had the ability to shed a tear when something touched his heart, he thanked God.

After the performance they wandered along in silence until they reached the Café de la Paix. "Coffee?" Dick enquired.

"Please!" She spoke shyly. As they found a table, Dick asked her name. "Laure," she replied hesitantly.

He wanted to know all about her, what had made her go on to the streets? In the Legion there had often been bands of prostitutes, camp followers, who moved every time the Company moved, who sheltered within the safety of the outposts. This he understood as it was part of the life of a Legionnaire. What he could not understand was this young girl who sat so quietly beside him. Why was she all alone in the big city?

The girl explained that her father was French and her mother Italian. They had been living in Cannes when, at the age of fourteen, she had been seduced and became pregnant. The family disowned her and she drifted down to Marseilles where the baby was still born. Destitute, she was picked up by a man who forced her to work in a brothel, where he could control both her and her earnings. Sometime later, Laure ran away to Paris where she became a registered prostitute, holding a Carte Blanche. As she explained this to Dick, she took the card from her bag to show him. On it was her name, place of birth – Cannes, date of birth 1906. She was twenty-four years old.

By now his companion was becoming more comfortable with the situation and began to chat away about herself and her friends. She told him that she must report periodically to the Prefecture for medical examination and that some of her friends had Cartes Rouges, meaning they had venereal disease.

Then she asked him candidly. "Would you like to live with me? You would not have to work. I have a nice flat and I can make a lot of money. Men really like me. You could protect me."

For a moment Dick was stunned. He had shown an interest in her but he could not see himself as a souteneur. Expecting her to laugh, he suggested it would be better for her to give up her present career and look for a job where she did not require protection. Looking serious, Laure asked for his address, telling him she would write to him in England when she had taken his advice. Instead, he made a mental note of her address.

It was a fine night and so they walked to La Nouvelle

Athene, a night-club that would stay open until dawn. They had a few drinks then, leaving the club at around 4am, they strolled down the Rue Pigalle to the corner of the Rue de Douai. Suddenly, they were surrounded by ten 'police mobile' on push-bikes. A group of about twenty civilians was being ushered along the pavement and it seemed that Dick and Laure were expected to join them.

"What the devil is going on?" Dick asked.

"Une rafle," Laure replied hoarsely, placing a restraining hand on his arm. "Keep away from me. You don't know me!" The girl slipped away to mingle with the others.

They were taken to the poste de police in the Rue de Douai. All passports and identity papers were checked. It was one of the periodic comb-outs of the streets in which the police hoped they would catch a few criminals. The first three men were allowed to go. The fourth man, who was about forty years old, was questioned at length and then made to strip naked, except for his socks. Eventually he was also told to leave but, as he started to pull on his trousers, a sharp-eyed officer demanded that he remove his socks. In them were small, folded packets which fell to the floor. "*De la coco!*" the policeman declared triumphantly as he scooped up the drugs.

At last it was his turn and Dick handed over the only papers he had on him, discharge papers from the Legion and a rail warrant to Calais. The police seemed reasonably satisfied but they checked with the Surete Generale before finally releasing him.

He waited around outside the police station for his companion but there was no sign of her. Then he took a quick look back inside the station, being careful not to draw attention to himself. Again he waited around outside and as it was already daylight he decided to leave. Making his way to the nearest Metro, he walked round the corner of the Rue Fontaine when Laure materialised from a doorway. Hand in hand they made their way to the Gare du Nord where he would catch his train for Calais.

For a moment he held her to him.

"Thank you, thank you for treating me as a human being, I will never forget you." Laure whispered, with tears in her eyes.

Smiling, he touched her cheek gently with his hand and, giving her a mock salute, he opened the door of the train and climbed aboard.

At Calais it was necessary for Dick to visit the vice-consulate to obtain a temporary passport enabling him to sail for Dover. He reached Victoria Station late at night, tired, dishevelled and with nowhere to go. The only people he knew in London were Harry Pearson and his son. Really, it would be an imposition to call either of those good people as he only knew of them through their letters. At this time of night they would hardly wish to welcome an unexpected guest. Deciding he would have to fend for himself, he settled down to sleep on a waiting room bench, hoping for better things in the morning.

He had barely closed his eyes before being shaken hard by the strong arm of the law. In no uncertain terms he was told he must leave his sanctuary in the huge station building. Outside it was freezing and the only way to keep warm was to walk. Walking meant thinking and he kept hearing the words of Captain Pechkoff drumming in his head: Une fois Legionnaire, toujours Legionnaire. In his mind's eye, he could see the Sahara. How he wished he could feel the sun. He had forgotten how the air in England had a penetrating damp. Also, he had forgotten the reserve of people who did not want to know a stranger.

For a couple of hours he walked, trying to decide if he would stay or go. He had just enough money to take him back to Paris and the French Foreign Legion, but was that what he really wanted? One discovery of life on the 'big outside' was already disturbing him, the amazing shades of simple truth. Hypocrisy was unknown in the Legion. He had come from a world where everything was black or white. If a Legionnaire did not like someone, they said so and, if asked, gave the reason why. Dick was frequently aware of insidious cankers at work in the conversations of people who were ready to gush extravagant compliments to a person's face and then blacken his character the minute he turned away.

Eventually, frozen and worn-out, he found himself in Trafalgar Square and a place to rest in the crypt of St. Martin in the Fields Church.

Things looked slightly better in the morning sunlight and so he scrapped his plans to return to France, deciding it was wrong to condemn England on the evidence of one dismal night. Besides, he was British. A card in a shop window offering rooms to let, took Dick to Holland Street, off Tottenham Court Road. Here to his delight he found an Italian landlady who was overjoyed to converse with a 'fellow countryman'. (This type of comment was to become common place with every language he spoke with the exception of his own tongue. Dick was so fluent in seven languages that he was always taken as a national. Strangely in English he still had the very slightest, indefinable accent.)

The next step was to look for employment but Dick had barely left the shelter of his new digs when he began to feel very ill. Managing to drag himself back to his room, he fell on to the bed lying there until several hours later when the landlady heard him shouting. Realising that something was very wrong the woman let herself in with the pass key and, taking one look at Dick, immediately sent for a doctor. A reoccurrence of malaria had struck without warning. Usually he knew if an attack was imminent and then, for a while, it would affect him every other day at about the same time. By taking a stiff drink about an hour before hand he would manage to keep his temperature down. On this occasion the doctor prescribed quinine and plenty of bed-rest.

Days later, with the need to earn money uppermost in his mind, Dick was walking purposefully down Tottenham Court Road. He had taken the precaution of having a double whisky in the Black Horse to ward off any more bugs. Unfortunately he had left it a little late to take his 'medicine' and just as he reached the corner of Store Street, he collapsed.

The policeman, who was called to the scene by passers-by, smelled the whisky and understandably arrived at the wrong conclusion. He took Dick back to the police station as a drunk. By an extremely lucky chance, a doctor had been called to look at a prisoner in the cells and noticing the detainee in passing, he realised this was a very sick young man. Within minutes Dick was being transferred to the Hospital for Tropical Diseases in Ensleigh Gardens.

At the hospital, the new patient was a man of mystery. He had no papers and his ramblings were in such a mix of languages that no-one could make the slightest sense of anything he said. In the morning, a huddle of doctors gathered round his bed clearly intent on riding his body of the malaria and any other obscure illness he might have contracted on his travels. They took numerous slides, smeared with his microbe packed blood, for the hospital students to examine at their leisure.

The staff nurse's insistence that he should supply her with details of his next of kin resulted in his giving the name and address of the only people he knew in England, the Pearsons. The Reverend Harry Pearson arrived at the hospital with his son who, Dick later discovered, was known as Mac to his family and friends. It was the first time they had all met, but both men had a knack of putting people immediately at their ease and of solving problems with little more than a quiet word. As his two visitors left the hospital, Reverend Pearson promised Dick he would find him a job.

Soon after he was released from the hospital, Dick received a letter from Harry Pearson suggesting they meet at the reverend's office in Euston. The job on offer was for an assistant housemaster at a school for delinquent boys situated in Basingstoke, Hampshire. Well-now, that's a turn-up for the books, he thought. There is not a lot I don't know about juvenile delinquents. Thinking about the job a little more seriously, he realised that at least these young lads would be given a fair chance if he took the post. He would listen to them and perhaps understand them better than most. Certainly he would do his damnedest to help them.

The more thought he gave to the school the more the prospect of working there became exciting. He had been offered a challenge which would pay good money and on top of which, food and lodging would be free. The school was situated in a large white house close to the centre of Basingstoke, a far cry from the Sahara Desert.

On his arrival at the school Dick was given a warm welcome and shown a pleasant bedroom with an adjoining sitting room that was to be his future home. This small apartment had the added advantage that it was close to the boy's dormitory. Outside there were extensive gardens to the back and front with a number of smaller outbuildings dotted around.

There were about twenty boys between the ages of fifteen and seventeen who would be in his care. All had been before the courts for minor offences but most of them were at the school because their parents had simply given up on them. Dick spent a long time studying the records of the inmates, convinced that they all had the potential to do well. He remembered his own unfortunate school days, the un-intentional escapades, the misunderstandings, the desperate loneliness and the fears born of his own defiant pride. His own stubbornness in the Legion spoke reams. He was determined to show these boys that their first duty was to themselves and give them the same chance that he was given by his captain at Colomb Bechar. Once they liked and respected themselves then so they would gain the respect of everyone else, including their peers.

Getting to know the boys proved reasonably simple as they were all fascinated by his past. Several gave up late passes to listen to modified stories of his exploits in the French Foreign Legion. None of them had travelled abroad and so he could keep their attention for long periods, telling them about Turkey, America, France, Italy, Greece and North Africa. There was an amazing improvement in the boys' knowledge of history and geography. Before long they were also showing an interest in learning to speak French. Dick was a man without any guile and without realising it, he had given many of his charges the one thing they needed, their very own hero to emulate.

Dick Cooper had been there, suffered the consequences and had risen above it. All this was in spite of, not because of!

From the first day that he joined the school, Dick preferred to take his meals with the boys rather than in the privacy of his own rooms. It was important to him and essential for them that a family atmosphere be established. There was a system of prefects in operation at the establishment and before long the new master discovered that the system was being misused. Younger boys were being intimidated and in some areas bullying was rife. Calling a meeting in the dining hall, Dick explained that, in future, prefects would be appointed on a rota basis and he made it quite clear that bullying would not be tolerated.

The following day Dick was summoned to the headmaster's study. The man sitting behind the huge desk was stooped and balding. Looking up as the assistant housemaster entered the room he gave a pleasant and welcoming smile. Dick was quite unprepared for the onslaught that followed. Still smiling, the man demanded to know why the new appointee had taken it upon himself to change the rules in regard to prefects. Paul Lovall had been at the school for several years and in that time he had trained his prefects to tell tales on the other boys. The man was operating a policy of fear and, as he let the smile drop from his face it was instantly replaced by shades of intimidating fury. Dick could understand a child being terrified by this red-faced demon who was, by then, shaking his finger in Dick's face.

The former Legionnaire silently stood his ground in the face of the tantrum being played out before him. Eventually, when the finger stopped wagging, Dick explained quietly that his terms of reference from Reverend Pearson were to obtain results by whatever methods he thought the best. Raising his voice slightly, Dick added with dignity, "I will be happy to consult you in future if that is your wish!"

That weekend, he took the boys into the countryside where he taught them to use a compass. They thoroughly enjoyed their day, using compass bearings to find coins left at strategic points by the master. It was a happy group that returned laughing and relaxed to the school that evening. It was quite obvious that Dick had gained their trust as well as their respect.

One Sunday afternoon as he sat writing a letter to Lieutenant Vecchioni, Dick glanced out of the window to see a senior boy leading a younger one up to the loft of a distant outbuilding. Leaving his letter unfinished, the master went to investigate. He was deeply concerned that the event he had just witnessed meant there was more bullying going on. The young lad had seemed very reluctant. Quietly he climbed the ladder and as he reached the level of the loft he knew what he was about to witness. Homosexual acts could not be tolerated. This was England in the 1930s and, by anyone's standards the boys were minors. In the same circumstances, heterosexual acts would not be tolerated either.

The boys were startled by his approach and looked at him with a mixture of fear and guilt on their faces. Dick had no wish to frighten them. He needed time to think. As he faced the boys he had no idea what to say or do. There was a long painful pause before he eventually spoke. Then, quietly telling the two offenders to rejoin the others, he returned to his own room to think.

In the Legion the act of homosexuality was well known. There were those who had joined to try and prove they were a male and escape from the doubts and fears they harboured about their own sexuality. Others could not tolerate the absence of women during long spells in the wilderness. To some extent this later problem was solved by the BMC, which stood for Bordel Militaire de Campagne, the military brothel.

The boys in his care were at an age to experiment in sex. Perhaps they should have expected this sort of thing to happen where youngsters were grouped together for continuous periods. He thought back to his own school days and realised there was no comparison. At their age he was fighting in the Dardanelles.

The questions and answers were becoming more and more complicated as he turned the matter over in his mind. Many of these boys had been abandoned by their families. These were children desperately in need of love and parental guidance. That doesn't make them homosexual, he thought. Undoubtedly there was a whole combination of things that needed to be taken into account, including the natural element. The only thing of which Dick could be sure was that if he was having a problem, then what were the boys themselves thinking at this moment?

The last thing he wished to do was to report the matter to

the headmaster but Dick was not qualified to deal successfully with the issue. After all, the headmaster was a trained professional. At least, he should have been professional. In effect, when he heard of the events, Mr. Lovall jumped up and down in a raging temper demanding that Dick cane the two boys involved, immediately. The housemaster calmly refused to take the cane that was being thrust at him and he tried to discuss the matter further with his superior.

"How dare you, how dare you refuse to take an order from me. You will be sacked unless you cane these boys." By now the man had completely lost control.

Again Dick refused to cane the boys. The headmaster was spluttering as he demanded to know if Dick condoned the act he had witnessed.

"Certainly I don't condone it, but I would like to understand more about the boys," the reply came quietly.

"It's not your job to understand. It is your job, it is an assistant master's job to give the cane. The rules say corporal punishment must be given." Paul Lovall was not used to being disobeyed by a subordinate.

The following day Mr. Lovall contacted the Reverend Pearson who, hearing half the story, gave the headmaster his full support. Dick was told that if he continued refusing to carry out the punishment, he would be dismissed. Accepting the verdict, Dick collected his salary plus a months pay in lieu of notice and with a heavy heart went to his room to pack.

13 Motivation

Back in London, Dick made for his old lodgings in Holland Street. The Italian landlady was delighted to see him again and insisted he should sleep on her couch until a room became available, hopefully in just a few days.

His severance pay from the school provided sufficient funds to tide him over for a while. Now was the time to stop and think carefully about his future. He was genuinely sorry to have left the school but there was nothing to be gained from a showdown with the head-teacher. Years of military training had taught him when to advance and when to retreat and this was certainly the latter of the two. However he could and did let the Reverend Pearson know the full facts in the hope the boys would get a better deal.

It was important to him that it had been his own decision to leave the job and he felt a certain satisfaction in knowing that from now on he was in control of his life. As far back as his own school years he had been obeying orders, or worse, obeying orders without question. Now, at last, he was his own master and would decide for himself the direction he would take.

Memories of the French Foreign Legion no longer called him back. Finally he had cut himself free of those apron strings. Vaguely he wondered about searching for his mother but dismissed the idea without a twinge of concern. More important was where would he like to live, Italy, or in Turkey, France, Morocco, America? No! His birth certificate said he was British and here he would stay. This was his home. So, he had established where!

The next question was what? What did he really want from life? The first thing to do was to find a new occupation. The tourists who thronged the West End of London provided the means. Thomas Cook and Son were delighted with his linguistic skills and welcomed him with open arms. Within twenty-four hours he was working as a guide and interpreter. A party of thirty bankers from Spain and Italy were in London for a conference and they needed a guide to show them and their families around London. The two languages were no problem to the newly appointed guide; unfortunately it was London that he didn't know. What a pity it wasn't Rome they wished to visit!

At 9am the following morning he introduced himself to the party of tourists before they all set off for St. Paul's Cathedral. Once inside the Cathedral, Dick began to relax. Someone had done the work for him: there were explanatory plaques everywhere. He just had to translate the information, glibly throwing in any other famous names he happened to notice.

His smooth flow of patter began to falter when the party reached Westminster Abbey. One persistent menace, the sort all guides dread, wanted to see the place where Queen Victoria was buried. Dick didn't have a clue where that might be but felt it would be unwise to say so. Consequently, he avoided his bete noire as much as possible while seeking out a face saving plaque. Chattering away to the group, first in Italian and then in Spanish, he invented stories about the people who lay in the Abbey. Still he was badgered for Queen Victoria. As they were leaving the Abbey he looked at the shrine of Edward the Confessor and decided it would have to do. It looked impressive enough for a queen so he pointed it out as such. Everyone seemed to accept the deception. Many of them grateful that their colleague had at last been silenced.

A coach tour had been organised for the afternoon and so, after an excellent lunch, they set off for Windsor Castle. Dick took the single seat near to the driver who was indicating places to him as they passed. Then the driver asked: "Have you told them Queen Victoria is buried in a mausoleum over there at Frogmore?" Dick glanced around guiltily; thank goodness no one seemed to have understood.

Evidently the bankers were all duly impressed with his ability as a guide and one of them, a director of the Arnuz Bank of Barcelona, subsequently asked Dick to accompany him and his family to Rome. This was a city he really knew something about, having spent a great many hours there on his way from Messina in 1916.

The party arrived at the Termini Station in Rome after a day and a night on the train. Dick barely had time to freshen up at the Hotel Nazionale before the family dragged him off to St. Peter's and the Vatican. On the second day they started a tour of the city's architectural showpieces. To the pure delight of their guide, each evening was spent at the opera. When the time came to part, they did so as friends. The family was heading to Naples to take a boat home to Barcelona while Dick, with his future again in doubt, returned to London.

Working as an independent guide had proved far more profitable than working for a tour operator. The main problem would be obtaining regular work. On the homeward voyage across the channel he came up with an idea. He had a number of cards printed describing himself as a guide and courier.

Armed with these he crossed the channel again without disembarking in France. On the voyage home he distributed the cards to tourists. Immediately he was engaged for two weeks by an American he had met in the ship's bar.

For a while he managed to pick up some interesting work by plying his cards on the cross channel ferries. He used all the routes: Dover/Calais, Newhaven/Dieppe, Southampton/Le Harve, Harwich/Hook of Holland and his favourite Folkestone/Boulogne. One by one the ferry captains became aware of his presence on board and he would be escorted from the boat and warned not to tout for business there again. Eventually the entire ferry fleet had banned him.

Between jobs he had two main hobbies. He loved listening to opera on gramophone records and the radio and he had become an inveterate letter writer, keeping in touch regularly with his brother and sister and half sister.

Wilf, who had recently moved to London, was in the throes of starting an Estate Agency business and he invited Dick to join him. Accepting the job mainly to help his brother get the venture off the ground, Dick dreaded the long boring days that unquestionably stretched ahead. As it happened, the boredom only lasted a few days just until the day when Wilf interviewed some young ladies for the post of secretary.

Doris was just seventeen years old and recently out of Convent school where she had learned 'Pitman's shorthand and typing to a very high standard.' A number of young ladies had applied for the vacancy but none could hold a candle to Doris for looks as well as ability. Of medium height, with lovely legs and a nice figure, Doris had an unhurried but efficient air about her. She took the interview in her stride and with a toss of light brown curls, saw off the opposition with her speed in both shorthand and typing.

Dick was mesmerised. This girl was nothing like any other he had met before. Beneath the quiet efficiency lay a shy disposition. Doris was the youngest child of elderly parents, and her sister was twenty years her senior. The girl had been a pupil at the Convent of the Sacred Heart in Bromley and had been over protected both at school and at home. Suddenly Wilf found it impossible to get his young brother out of the office.

Appointing himself Doris' protector in chief, Dick insisted on escorting her to and from her home and the office. The young girl was charmed by the attention he lavished on her and before long they were dating regularly. Although there were sixteen years between their ages, neither of them noticed, particularly Doris as this young man was five years younger than her sister, Rose. Dick was young in outlook and, for all his experience, at times incredibly naïve. While Doris had a reserved side to her nature she also had a very quick sense of humour far beyond her years. Their backgrounds were different in the extreme so that quite amazingly they made exceptional partners. In no time Dick proposed and they were married at a quiet ceremony in Bromley in 1931.

They managed to find a small flat in Brixton and spent many happy hours making it into a home. With the odd piece of second hand furniture, hand-sewn sheets and pillowcases, orange boxes transformed into stools and kitchen cupboards, the pair of them were deliriously happy. Outside the cosy nest they were building, life was becoming more and more difficult. The slump had stamped despair on almost every face they saw. Wilf had decided to cut his losses and move abroad to find greener pastures with the result that both the newly weds were out of work. Strangely enough there were still people around with money to spend on continental holidays and consequently, Dick was able to pick up work from a number of travel agencies.

Between these trips a letter had arrived for Dick from Lieutenant Vecchioni. He wrote:-

My Dear Cooper,

I was glad to get your news and your letter amused me very much. I found in it once more the good humour of the old campaigner and that pride which those who have served in the Legion always retain. The Battalion celebrated the Camerone this year at Marrakech. Once more the Company got the first prize. The fete was, as usual, moving, joyous and cordial.

A month later we went on path-making work at Amizmiz. We have another three months of it, after that back to Marrakech for a month and then the withdrawal of the 1ˢᵗ Battalion from Ouar Zazat and this is the plan of our work mapped out til the end of 1931.

Rosik is due for repatriation next September. I showed him your letter which excited his home-sickness and longing for the future joys of his native town. He did not dare to ask to be remembered to you but I know he wanted to and I gladly do so for him.

Au revoir, Cooper old chap. You have my best wishes and I hope you will have good luck in your new life. I keep my 'tutoiement' for you because you were a good Legionnaire and I shake you warmly by the hand.

Vecchioni.

Lieutenant Vecchioni had included the address of Lieutenant Djintcharadze and a few months later, Djin arrived in England. It was a happy reunion when the Lieutenant called at their flat and Dick proudly introduced Doris to him. Over a couple of bottles of wine, the two men talked well into the night, recalling old friends and times gone by. Eventually they made a bed up on the floor for Djin as it was much too late for him to leave. That was to be the last time they met. Djin returned the next day to his battalion in Morocco.

Doris was expecting a baby and so they found a slightly larger flat in Victoria Road, Clapham. They were both looking forward to the birth of their child but Dick was also somewhat bemused at the thought of the coming event. He found it so hard to accept that not only had he found a beautiful wife but he was also about to become a father. Life seemed to have a permanent rosy glow and the twelve years he had spent in the Legion Etranger seemed little more than a distant memory.

The birth of his son brought Dick Cooper back down to earth with a bang. The baby was born at home on the 21st February 1932 and named Richard Arthur, after his father and his grandfather. That evening, Doris became seriously ill and was rushed to the hospital. Meanwhile, Dick was left holding the baby in the literal sense. There was no help in the form of home visits by midwives or health visitors. The father had not the slightest idea how to care for a new-born baby. Puppies – yes, eagles – yes, mules – yes, but babies – help!!! He was desperately worried about Doris and terrified that he might do something wrong in caring for the baby. A neighbour from the top floor offered to help him and he left the child with her for a short period while he dashed to a bookshop in Lavender Hill and purchased a manual on child-care. Turning on his heel he raced back to the house, cursing himself for leaving the child with a near stranger.

Satisfying himself that the neighbour was indeed a kindly, motherly woman who had raised a family of her own, Dick felt able to leave the child again and go to the hospital. Only as he went through the doors of the hospital emergency wing did he realise how terrified he had been since the emergency had occurred. At the back of his mind he kept hearing voices, voices telling him he had always lost those he loved. At the desk he was told to wait as the doctor was with his wife. Dick sat on the edge of his chair, eyes closed, head bent in silent prayer. Once again, in his mind he could see Lucy. He had never doubted that Lucy was always there for him but what of his wife and his child?

A ward sister approached, looking serious. "We hope to save her." She said quietly. Doris had puerperal fever due to an infection contracted during childbirth. Dick insisted on staying at her bedside until they eventually announced that she was out of danger. As soon as he was sure Doris was safe, he raced back to the neighbour to satisfy himself that all was well with his son. Taking a brief respite, he couldn't help thinking – 'It was never this tough in the French Foreign Legion.'

For three weeks Doris remained in hospital while Dick cared for the baby. He paid a visit to their doctor who had been conspicuous by his absence. "It was just unfortunate," said the man, "that it was my first experience of a delivery on my own!"

Once Doris was able to care for the baby it became essential that Dick should find gainful employment. He decided to try his business cards on the ferry boats once more, convinced the captains would have either left or forgotten about him. For a while he managed to escape their attention and brought home some much needed cash. Then the same old process started and one by one the captains banned him from their boats. The last to ban him was the captain of the Folkestone/Boulogne route and leaving the harbour behind him; Dick climbed the hill through the old town and sat on the clifftop. As he gazed across the vast expanse of water to the French coast, again the memories flooded into his mind. There were always so many memories, so many places he had seen, so many people he had met, so many years. Suddenly he stood up, smiling, full of energy. He was going home to his waiting wife and child. Tomorrow was another day.

Between jobs, Dick had continued his long and detailed correspondence with friends. He enjoyed writing and found himself writing an occasional short story. One of these stories was eventually published in a book of fifty short stories about the Great War. Then the publishing company Jarrolds showed an interest in Dick's experiences in the French Foreign Legion. Although he was happy to spend his spare time writing, Dick needed to find paid employment as the bills were mounting up. Searching through the newspapers, he came across an advertisement for a demonstrator required by Singer Thermoplastic Products. He had never heard of such things but decided to apply anyway.

A few days later, a letter from Singers invited him to attend an interview at an office in Blackheath where he met the two Austrian-Jewish brothers who were running the firm. Although they expressed concern at his lack of experience, the brothers decided to take Dick on for a trial period. The next day he had to travel to Folkestone to watch another demonstrator at work in a large sea-front hotel selling Bakelite egg beaters, egg separators and toilet seats. Without any further training, Dick was sent to give a demonstration of the products at an exhibition in Alexandra Palace. He surprised himself at the large numbers of people that he managed to attract to the stall; some were intrigued by his accent and looked doubtful when he said he was English.

Reasonably pleased with the success of their new recruit, the brothers then arranged for him to demonstrate their wares at various large stores in London. Eventually they sent him to try his sales technique at an exhibition in the Palais du Cinquantenaire in Brussels after which, they managed to provide him with intermittent periods of work.

In 1933 the publishing house of Jarrolds accepted Dick's book of 'Twelve Years in the French Foreign Legion' for publication. The money he received in royalties on the book was a very welcome addition to the family coffers but it wouldn't last forever. Soon he had to return to the tourist trade.

The first job he was offered was to accompany a party of sightseers to Paris. Finding himself at a loose end for a few hours he decided to look up Laure. He didn't expect to have much luck as she was sure to have moved on; nevertheless he had often wondered what had happened to her and whether she had taken his advice. At the address she had given him he was told she was at work. A little early to be on the streets, he thought. As he walked away from the house the neighbour called him back. "Try the restaurant of the Galerie Lafayette, between twelve and one."

Promptly at noon, Dick entered the restaurant and ordered lunch. Looking around the room he saw a group of girls squeezed around a corner table, laughing and chatting noisily. Attracted by their friendly fun, Dick's eyes kept straying to the group until he suddenly realised that Laure was seated among them. Writing a quick note, he passed it to waitress to give to Laure. The girl looked up smiling and leaving the group came over to his table. It was quite obvious that she was happy. She had grown up and her manner was pleasant and assured. She had certainly taken his advice and although it had been tough at first, she had never looked back. Laure was a supervisor in the ladies dress department, having made rapid progress though the ranks. She positively glowed when Dick showed her the photographs of his baby son, explaining that she was getting married shortly and was looking forward to starting a family of her own.

Returning to England, Dick decided it was time he put a little security into their lives. Doris, or Dolly as he had taken to calling his wife, had become a very practical and efficient housewife and mother developing skills in cooking, sewing and household accounts. Nevertheless he knew that she worried about the times when he was out of work and he was determined to do something about that. Early the next morning he joined the queue at the labour exchange and discovered he had a talent that was much in demand. The Continental Telephone Exchange was short of linguists, particularly French speaking. His application was accepted and he passed the Post Office test with flying colours. Within twenty-four hours Dick had reported to the Clerkenwell Telephone Exchange for initial training, then transferring to CX (Continental Telephone Exchange) for training in international telephone procedures.

After taking a Civil Service examination at Burlington House, Dick served a probationary period and became a fully-fledged Civil Servant in the year of 1935. Respectability personified, a British Civil Servant! Part of him wanted to explode with laughter and the other part was incredibly proud of his own achievement.

Now he would do his travelling over the telephone lines. Although he had been employed to speak French, he was assured that it would not be very long before he would get to use his other languages, speaking to people across the world. Most of the time he would be required to work in the evenings or during the night, which would give him time to be with his son and Dolly. He could not believe his luck.

Occasionally Dick's thoughts would turn to his father, wondering just what it would have taken to have impressed the man. Realising that these thoughts were nothing more than empty daydreams, he tried to put them behind him; it was too late now his father was no longer around for him to please.

Dick Cooper had a front seat during the abdication crisis of 1936. King Edward VIII often came through to CX to speak to Mrs Simpson after her unhappy flight to France. The King later wrote in his memoirs that he nearly hurled the receiver against the wall because he could not make sense of what Mrs Simpson was saying to him. He mentioned particularly the call from the Hotel du Grand Cerf, at Evreux, in the Department of Eure. The problem had nothing to do with Dick, who was actually monitoring the call periodically without any interference. The particular call to which the King referred was from a coin box at the hotel and it was common knowledge that the French operators were listening for any royal calls and no doubt more than one eavesdropped, first at Rouen and then Paris. That was the reason for the interference.

Dick never revealed the subject matter of those calls to anyone including Dolly. Even in today's climate when the halls and corridors are running alive with 'mercenary moles,' I could not imagine my father ever revealing the secrets of the Duke and Duchess!

At the time of the Spanish Civil War, which broke out in July 1936, Dick was on the Barcelona direct line dealing with a call from a newspaperman, who was putting over his copy. Suddenly they heard a bomb explosion and then there was silence. CX had finished with Spain for a long time.

Next came the uneasy period of peace that preceded World War II. This was a time when CX provided the vital link with the troubled cities of Europe. The calls to and from the continent reached unprecedented levels and the exhausted members of staff at the exchange were constantly under pressure to man all the lines.

Returning home early one morning, Dick met the postman on the steps of the house and was handed a letter bearing a French stamp. Exhausted from his night's work, Dick peered at the writing on the envelope. Deciding he didn't know whom the letter was from, he tossed it onto the hall table as he headed for the kitchen and a much-needed cup of coffee. Later in the day he turned the letter over in his hands, still trying to guess the identity of the sender. When he did open it, Dick found it contained bad news. The writer was a Municipal Counsellor in Nice who was advising him that his sister Daisy was in hospital. She was suffering from nervous exhaustion and needed his help.

Arranging to take some of the holiday he was owed at work, Dick left immediately for Nice. His sister's husband, who had been suffering with tuberculosis, had recently died. Daisy had collapsed as a result of the shock and the strain of nursing him. When Dick reached Nice, the counsellor explained that she had managed to contact his mother and had suggested that the woman should visit her daughter. "Which mother?" Dick asked, surprised that his stepmother should show any interest in Daisy. "Madam de Wrobleski." the reply was abrupt with unspoken irritation.

Dick had lived with the ghost of his mother for so long that it came as a complete shock to be told he might meet her face to face at last. He had never known this woman who had abandoned him and his brother and sister, when he was just a baby. He was surprised to discover that his sister had been in touch with their mother for some time. Apparently the woman was rich, having inherited a great deal of money and property when de Wrobleski had died. Her husband had owned many buildings in Constantinople and had also kept a yacht. On his death, his possessions had been shared between his wife and two daughters, Dick's half sisters Wanda and Zoska.

Dick found it strange. If his mother had been in touch with Daisy then she must know of his whereabouts and yet she had made no effort to contact him. Certainly it had nothing to do with a lack of funds so it had to be a lack of interest.

A couple of weeks later, Dick made arrangements to take his sister home with him. During this time there had been no sign of Madam Wrobleski.

From the day she arrived in England, Daisy was unhappy. Although she was British by birth she could not speak a word of the English language and made no effort to try. Dolly went out of her way to make her sister-in-law comfortable but there was nothing she could do about the weather, which was the subject of continuous complaint. They were not surprised when their guest suddenly decided she wanted to return to France and, within days, she left for Paris.

During his sister's visit he learned a little more about his half sisters. Wanda was married to a German engineer and Zoska to a Belgian Consul. Both sisters had been married before and, like their mother they had left their respective families and, after divorces, had married again.

Just a few days after Daisy's departure for Paris, Dick received a letter from his mother, the only one she ever wrote to him. Addressing him as 'My very dear son', she gave her reasons for running away from his father, blaming everyone and everything except herself. Finally she expressed a wish to meet him and with mixed feelings he made arrangements to meet her off the boat at Folkestone.

Only when he arrived at Folkestone did Dick realise that he hadn't the slightest idea of how he would recognise his mother. He had never so much as seen a photograph of her and, to his knowledge she would experience the same problem. Explaining the situation to an immigration officer, Dick stationed himself at the man's side while the passports were being checked. Towards the end of the queue of passengers was an elderly grey haired lady who was leaning heavily on a walking stick. Instinctively he knew it was his mother. As the petite woman came closer, he could see a resemblance to Daisy.

"*Bonjour Madam*," he said. "I am Bebo."

As they shook hands formally, he knew that they would never be more than strangers. The visit was short and they parted, as they met, with politeness and dignity. They were never to meet again.

A few days later, the anti-climax of the meeting with his mother was forgotten as he unexpectedly bumped into a very old friend. Young Richard had been suffering with a chesty cough and each time it seemed to be clearing up, it would start all over again. The local doctor seemed to be at a loss and so Dick finally took his son to Great Ormond Street Hospital.

For sometime they sat and waited for the doctor to finish his rounds on the wards, then, as the doctor approached, Dick jumped to his feet instantly recognising Doctor John Hartigan from the Seaman's Hospital in Cardiff. He had been no more than a boy himself when he had last seen Doctor Hartigan. The two men chatted over old times and Dick delighted in introducing his young son to the doctor. The little boy's cough eventually being checked out and dealt with, almost as an after thought.

Dolly gave birth to their second child, Patricia Anne, in April 1938, this time in the safety of Lewisham Hospital. Two months later I was baptised by the Reverend Harry Pearson at the church of St Pancras in London. The two families had always been in close contact and Harry's son, Mac, his daughter, Nellie, and his wife, Evelyn became my godparents.

Nine months later, peace hung on a slender thread. Chamberlain had gone to meet Mussolini in Rome and Dick Cooper was responsible for the subsequent telephone links throughout the night. From 7pm to 8am the next day he was kept busy putting calls through to Government departments and newspaper offices. Arriving home the next morning, he was feeling exhausted. Then he started to feel very ill for no apparent reason. Lowering his weary body into an armchair he called for Dolly, only to realise that she would be taking Richard to school. Suddenly he was racked with a fit of coughing and blood spurted from his lungs. Pushing a handkerchief to his mouth he made his way to the nearest doctor's surgery and within a very short time he had been rushed into Lewisham Hospital.

The doctors diagnosed Haemoptysis and by the time Dolly had been contacted and brought to the hospital, a priest was administering the Last Sacrament. Members of the nursing staff were obviously annoyed with the constant interruptions by the priest, who they thought was a little premature with his prayers and who was continually getting in their way. Taking in the scene at a glance, a very worried Dolly quietly told the priest to leave, only to be vehemently advised by him that she wouldn't go to heaven. "At this moment I really don't care. LEAVE!" she very forcefully instructed the man.

Meanwhile, Dick had suddenly sat up in bed and reached for cigarettes and matches. "Are you quite mad?" enquired the nurse.

He continued to light the cigarette and when it became too blood stained to smoke any further, he put it out and lit another. He couldn't explain why he was doing such a thing; he just felt a compelling urge which he had to obey. There was no sensible explanation. He couldn't discuss his actions with anyone, including his terrified wife. At the time he just knew it was essential that he should light a cigarette. A doctor came rushing into the side-ward only to be told by his patient, "I am fine now, thank you!"

As quickly as it had started, the bleeding stopped. No one knew what had triggered the problem and not a thing was found after a detailed investigation was carried out. Likewise, Dick was never able to explain why, when he was feeling so ill and in a state of collapse, did he suddenly feel so impelled to sit up and smoke a cigarette. Eventually he had to put it down to a mystery of life which, on the odd occasion, he would try unsuccessfully to fathom out.

By the time he returned to CX, Europe's torment was reflected in the busy switchboards. Calls were coming from every direction; diplomats, businessmen, newspaper correspondents, staff in offices at Whitehall, from families in Britain frantically trying to contact relatives abroad and from British subjects hurrying home from the expanding tide of the German invasion.

Meanwhile, the censors had taken control of the London CX. No calls were going through without their permission. All telephone messages from GHQ in France to the War Office in London had to go through the exchange in the early days of the war and the operators were among the best-informed people in the country.

Due to age, his expertise and his fluency in languages, Dick was placed in a reserved occupation at 'continental.' While there were many who would be grateful for the opportunity to stay in England, Dick was champing at the bit, convinced he could do far more for the war effort out in the field. He was after all a trained soldier with many years on his service record to prove it. It never occurred to him that he was by now forty years old.

It was the final sentence of the Prime Minister's broadcast to the nation that motivated him into action.

"It is the evil things we shall be fighting against - brute force, bad faith, injustice, oppression and persecution - and against them I am certain that right will prevail."

Dick Cooper was going to take a hand in that fight regardless of age, occupation or any other obstacle.

14 Notwithstanding

The period of the phoney war came to an end early in 1940. Each German victory extinguished another light on the CX switchboard, indicating that yet another circuit had been lost. There was a call from the Brussels Exchange to say they had to get out and would smash the exchange before they left. Explosions and the sounds of girl operators sobbing could be heard on the Amsterdam line before that circuit went dead. Antwerp was next followed by Ostend and then it was the turn of Paris.

Dick had the feeling he was personally letting all these people down. He should be out there; he should be fighting this war, not stuck in a telephone exchange which could be successfully manned by a non-combatant.

Then he had a bit of luck, which gave him the very chance he had been looking for. He was putting calls through to Bordeaux, the last link with Europe, when he overheard two British officers talking. The one at the London end, speaking from a Welbeck number, said they were having problems finding suitable people for undercover work behind enemy lines.

At last! That's for me he thought, and when the call finished he got through to the Welbeck exchange and asked for the address of the telephone number. They refused to give it to him as it was listed under ex-directory. The only way he would be able to obtain the address was if one of the supervisors at his exchange would ask on his behalf. Before he could give any further thought to all the options, once again fate took a hand. The very next night the duty supervisor was taken ill and Dick was asked to take over. Within five minutes he had obtained the address he wanted.

Bright and early the next morning he was boldly knocking on the front door of the 'recruiting centre for secret agents.' The officer who opened the door was visibly shaken when Dick introduced himself as a potential candidate for subversive activities.

After some very careful and detailed checks, the 'powers that be' decided that Dick could prove extremely useful to them. He was sent to meet Thomas Cadet, the former BBC correspondent in Paris, and he was later interviewed at the War Office by Captain Gielgud, the brother of Sir John Gielgud. Then they were forced to weather a particularly frustrating period, untangling the mass of red tape that was Civil Service paperwork, eventually obtaining his release from the reserved occupation status. At last Dick was accepted as a member of MI1 (X) which later became well known as the Special Operations Executive, S.O.E.

Meanwhile, Doris and the children had been evacuated from London. Initially they were sent to Reigate but they returned for a short period when things quietened down. Before long they were off again, this time to a little village in Northamptonshire where they spent the rest of the war, most of it waiting desperately for news of Dick who had returned to a life of a daredevil, on this occasion as a secret agent for the British.

The school for the initial training of secret agents was at Wanborough Manor, near Guildford, Surrey. For the latest recruit, Morse code and the use of explosives presented no problems. It was the early morning runs over the Hog's Back that Dick found to be the killer. The years had been sneaking past without him noticing and he was shocked to find that the fitness he had always enjoyed was suddenly eluding him. Thankfully it took little more than a fortnight to have him feeling better and only another week or two before he was completely back in shape.

The course intensified and Dick was sent to a rambling house in the wilds of Ayrgyllshire to learn about the various methods of destruction, from the silent killing of a sentry to the razing of a factory. Then things became even more spine-tingling with his first flight from Ringway airfield including his maiden parachute jump. At the airfield the group of novices were taken to the parachute room where they watched the parachutes being carefully folded by W.A.A.F. girls. Next they were due to be given some theoretical instruction but, as usual, the timing was out and the aircraft was ready for take off, so they were told they would receive all the instruction they needed once they were in the air.

Members of the motley group boarded the Whitley aircraft and sat in silence as the dispatcher explained the procedure. Each man was to sit on the edge of the hole, with legs dangling into space, watching for the red light to turn to green indicating that it was time to jump. Everyone listened carefully. They had all heard of Roman candles - the 'chutes that failed to open.

For a moment, Dick thought longingly of his reserved occupation and mentally kicked himself for giving it up so willingly. Then, as the dispatcher touched his shoulder, giving the thumbs up, the man shouted "Jump!" Dick was sweating profusely and his heart was thumping rapidly but he jumped.

For a second his mind went blank and then he felt a jerk as the parachute opened and he said a silent prayer of thanks. Looking down he could see a white circle on the ground and close to it an ambulance stood at the ready. For a moment he was apprehensive and then excitement surged through every part of his body. He was alive again, alert, fascinated and thrilled at the prospect of the days and months to come. He was enjoying the sensation of floating and swaying gently towards the earth when a voice, stentorian through a megaphone, blared: "Put your knees up and pull on the rigging! Turn now!"

Before the voice had stopped, Dick was on his feet in the middle of the circle, collapsing his 'chute while watching the others floating down to earth. They were all ready for another go and full of confidence until, once again, it was their turn to jump and the fear returned. This was a natural fear that would always return at that crucial moment before he jumped from an aircraft.

The final touch to his 'education' was at the Special Training School 36, set up in a secluded house called Booeman's, at Beaulieu on the edge of the New Forest. It was at Beaulieu that the purpose of the training was really brought home to the prospective agents. Here they perfected their cover stories, took on their new identities and learned to identify the various German ranks, weapons and transport.

As their training finished, the men and women were given leave before going into active service. Many of these people would not return from their missions; others would become famous heroes and heroines of their time; one or two simply would never make the grade but the majority would, one day, quietly return to mundane jobs in Civvy Street.

In civilian clothing once again, Dick made his way to Northamptonshire where Doris bombarded him with questions, none of which he was allowed to answer. He simply said that his job was hush-hush, he would be going away and that if there were any unexpected problems he would communicate through the Reverend Pearson. The most difficult part was to say his goodbyes to his family, not knowing when - or if, they would meet again. For a moment he held them all close and then, closing the door quietly behind him, he left for the unknown.

It was May 1941 when Dick was commissioned as a Second Lieutenant in the General List. Towards the end of June, he was on his way to Algeria via Gibraltar aboard the aircraft carrier Furious. His instructions were to carry out a programme of sabotage, propaganda and to organise the diversion of ship's cargoes. It was his service in the French Foreign Legion that had persuaded them to send him into North Africa on a mission. As it turned out he was the only Secret Agent to be landed in Algeria during the war.

A rowing boat crew deposited Dick on the Algerian coast and he made his way to Oran to start his work, making the first of many contacts and organising subversive activities. From there he travelled to Algiers once again setting up the necessary organisation. Deciding that his best option for establishing a semi-permanent base would be in Oran, he returned there and arranged a meeting with the help of a Polish Lieutenant whose name had been supplied to him by British Intelligence.

Unfortunately, Lieutenant Polanski was a double agent and, consequently, he arranged for a Lieutenant Schalemberg of the Deuxieme Bureau (French Intelligence) to accompany him to the planned meeting in the Café de Paris. The events that followed had all the ingredients of a classic espionage betrayal and Dick was inevitably arrested for spying.

At that time Algeria was ruled by the Vichy French and, under armed escort, Dick was taken to the Chateau Neuf Military Prison so familiar to him in his Legion days. A French guard hustled him along the winding corridors until finally stopping at an open door, motioning to Dick that he should step inside the cell. Stopping just inside the door to look around, Dick was suddenly propelled forward by a vicious kick landed at the base of his spine. His head struck the opposite wall with force and as the door clanged shut, he slid unconscious to the concrete floor.

There was a blackness shot through with swirling flashes of light, but the light spread no illumination. The light was in his whirling brain, aching and aching. Pain was everywhere, in his head, his back and down through his legs. Opening his eyes, lightning flashed across his eyeballs, lightning shots of agony. Putting a feeble hand to his head, he could feel that it was sticky and obviously he was bleeding. He tried to struggle to his feet but he couldn't move. Fear clutched at his heart. Was his spine fractured? He believed he must be paralysed. Putting out a hand he touched the wall, it was wet. He knew the floor was wet and slimy and he could feel the damp that had penetrated his clothes.

Many hours passed and eventually Dick managed to raise himself on his hands. He crawled round the cell painfully but at least he was not paralysed as he had at first thought. Finding a stone slab, he crawled upon it. There were no blankets and he was so cold, so incredibly cold. For a while he dozed fitfully and when he next opened his eyes he thought he was still in the Legion. Before him he saw the words: Jamais deux, sans trois.

For a moment he blinked furiously, trying to clear the haze before his eyes. Dizziness came and went, returning every time he tried to focus. He felt physically sick and giddiness continued to wash over him in waves. He closed his eyes tight and the feeling of nausea eased. Time passed and again he tried to open his eyes, this time managing to focus on the tightly closed door. Turning slowly he gazed around the cell until his eyes became accustomed to the half light. Slowly recognition of his surroundings began to penetrate his befuddled mind and his eyes alighted on his own name carved into the wall. Memories flooded into his aching head as he read the name of his friend, Schneider, and beneath it his own second signature with the date 1926. Below which were written the familiar words, jamais deux, sans trois.

For days they kept him locked up without human contact and then without warning another prisoner entered his cell to bring a mess tin of watery soup and beans. As he took the tin, Dick felt something else being pushed into his hand and his sense of touch told him it was a cigarette and a match. From then on he had a single daily meal of soup and beans.

He lost all sense of time and after a while devised mental exercises to keep his mind active. Between the exercises he would think of Dolly and the children but the pain of their separation would threaten to weaken his defences and he would start to pace his cell with military precision, determined to be strong for himself and his family. Occasionally he would experience flights of fancy when he could see and speak to Lucy. Always, after these comforting visitations, his resolve would strengthen.

When the day came for him to leave the cell, he walked unsteadily but with determination despite the fact his injuries were seriously infected and in need of attention. Given time to take a bath, Dick did what he could to patch up the wound on his head. He was then interrogated for several hours before being taken to a room where two other prisoners, De Gaulists, were being held. The two men, Michel de Camaret and Dr. Lion, helped him to clean up his head wound which was again oozing puss into his matted hair. While they worked on him they gave him news about the progress of the war and then supplied him with most of their food, knowing he would be going back to solitary confinement until such time as he confessed to being a British spy.

Luckily he had managed to ditch his forged livret maritime and identity papers during the confusion at the time of his arrest. Throughout his imprisonment, Dick had stuck to his prepared story that he was a member of the Royal Corps of Signals in France. He had been cornered by the German advance and had escaped by way of a boat from the port of Marseilles.

For a while they doubted his story and Dick was informed that he would stand trial with other agents including British, French and Germans. If he was found not guilty then he would be freed or alternatively sent to and internment camp. A verdict of guilty of espionage would ensure a death sentence and Dick would be shot.

A choice of legal representatives was offered to the prisoners and Monsieur Perrot and Mademoiselle Susanne Koehl agreed to represent Dick and inform the British authorities of his whereabouts.

It was late in September 1941 that Dolly received a letter from the War Office.

Dear Madam,

I understand that you have not had news regarding your husband for some time and, owing to the fact that communications between individuals are very difficult and subject to considerable delay at present, I am instructed to inform you that he is in normal health.

Lieutenant Colonel E. C. Whetmore

This was only one of the many communications that Doris Cooper was to receive during those months and years of the war. The one that stated her husband was – *'missing, believed killed in action'* - being among the most memorable.

With the help of his counsel Dick managed to persuade his captors that his cover story was indeed true. His knowledge of the various telephone exchanges throughout Europe was convincing and eventually, after five months in a filthy jail and many of those months in solitary confinement, confirmation of his cover story finally made it through channels. Not that it had all been bad for, never one to be idle, he had managed to thoroughly upset his captors on several occasions with his pranks, including feigning death and terrifying an Arab orderly when he came back as a ghost.

However, freedom was to prove elusive and he was released from one prison, only to be thrown into another. This time it was the Laghouat Internment Camp, far south on the edge of the Sahara.

He arrived at the camp at 1am on Christmas morning 1941, remembering another Christmas he had spent in prison, thirty years before when he was twelve years old.

Thankfully he was now able to send information home to England himself by way of the Red Cross and eventually Dolly received news of his actual whereabouts. Like so many other wives and mothers, Dolly busily made up food parcels out of the meagre rations available, knitted socks from wool obtained by unpicking other garments and helped the children to write and illustrate letters to their absent father.

It would be impossible to tell here in these pages the full story of the men of the Laghouat camp. A story to compare with so many others about the service men and women imprisoned in camps during the last war. It is doubtful that any of those camps were more escape proof than Laghouat, not even Colditz. Even if the physical defences could be pierced, a European escapee faced a trek of 300 miles of Arab country where his presence without proper clothes and a knowledge of Arabic would be immediately discovered.

Laghouat camp itself stood white, remote and menacing, in the insignificant village bearing the same name, on the desert side of the Saharan Atlas Mountains. The nearest railhead at Djelfa was fifty miles away. The closest town, some forty miles distant, was the walled city of Ghardaia. To the south was the range of mountains called the Big Occidental Erg and to the West, Monts des Ksour, the Djebel Amour and the Monts des Ouled Nail (the land of the dancing girls). Three hundred miles to the north was the coast. The camp stood on a barren plain with just a few palm trees breaking the monotony. Water was scarce and beyond Ghardaia stretched a thousand miles of undulating yellow-brown Sahara burning its way towards the central African jungles.

Needless to say that by the time Dick arrived at the internment camp an escape tunnel was already underway. Ignoring all the difficulties and dangers with a supreme contempt, the inmates were busy digging their way out.

At first Dick was somewhat peeved to hear about the tunnel as he felt he had a greater chance of escaping on his own. With an active camp escape committee it was impossible to work as an individual as this could endanger other attempts and so the new arrival had no choice but to acquiesce.

The day that Dick was shown the tunnel he realised just how desperately crazy the scheme was. The plan had evolved just two months earlier when the men discovered a sealed cellar under one of the huts. Quite simply they decided to dig a tunnel southwards right under the camp to a point just under the outside wall a distance estimated to be 180 feet (later proved to be 192 feet.)

The problems involved in getting the project underway included a lack of suitable tools. Two bread knives had to suffice as digging implements. They had no surveying instruments and no materials for shoring up the sides and roof. Finally they needed to move the earth away unobtrusively

218

while also providing some form of light and ventilation.

Working in the tunnel was always referred to as 'playing poker.' The ingenuity of the internees knew no bounds and lighting was at times diverted from the main supply and at other times it was provided by candles. A latrine trench was dug outside at right angles to the tunnel and a ventilation shaft duly installed.

Sweat poured off the men and grit, dust and earth ingrained their fingers, palms, knees and toes eventually clogging every pore of their bodies. They worked in shifts with everyone taking their turn. Most of them suffered from varying degrees of claustrophobia but one by one they overcame their fears and got on with the job in hand.

Seven months of work around the clock found the prisoners with worn-away knives and a usable tunnel. The 6th of June was chosen for the escape and thirty men and officers including Dick made their getaway in batches of three leaving at half-hourly intervals.

The night before they left the camp the former Legionnaire gave the escape team some tips on survival in the desert. Nevertheless, plagued by the scarcity of water and the hostility of the Arabs, most were caught within three days and a couple of days later Dick re-joined them.

Due to his never-ending energy and unwavering courage in planning a variety of disruptive activities around the prison a decision was taken to transfer Dick to the Chambaran Internment Camp near Grenoble in France. The camp commandant willingly handed over his own 'personal nightmare' to the Italo-German Armistice Commission who arranged an escort for Dick's relocation in France.

The first stage of the journey took him by boat to Marseilles and the Fort St Jean, standing as ever, proudly at the entrance of the Vieux Port. There they threw him into a cell, unaware of his previous association with the place or the hope he that he gained from being in familiar surroundings.

Amazingly, there had been no formal arrangements for his transfer from the port to the Chambaran camp but, possibly as a matter of respect for his reputation, he was given a personal escort of five guards to take him, by tram, to the Gare St. Charles on route for Lyon. The six men lined up solemnly in a queue in the Cannebiere. Dick, who was wearing a British battledress, found the people around him smiling encouragingly. There was no doubt he was among some friends.

When the tram arrived, guards and prisoner marched aboard in a solid phalanx. The tram was crowded and they were forced to stand in a conspicuous group, on the platform. As Dick peered over the shoulders of the guards, he could see more smiles on the faces of the French people. In this atmosphere he could almost taste freedom. The conductress went round for the fares and on her way slipped a packet of sweets in the prisoner's hand, nodding as he smiled his thanks. Suddenly an elderly man shouted:

"*Vive l'Angleterre!*"

A second man took up the cry.

"*Vive Churchill!*"

The call spread and mounted up and down the tram until it became a chant.

"*Vive l'Angleterre! Vive Churchill! Vive de Gaulle!* "

Dick was laughing silently as he glanced at the guards who were looking around uneasily. He could see the captain was scared and next minute the man ordered the tram to be stopped. The brave conductress snapped that they could only stop at the designated places. The crowd laughed.

A passenger rang the bell and the tram started to slow down. Up went the shout: "Let's all get off." There was a roar of laughter and in a solid body the French men and women rose from their seats and rushed to the platform, all the time they were grinning at Dick in encouragement. By this time the guards were hanging onto Dick's arms with such force that he thought they would tear from their sockets, he was helpless. For a moment the guards seemed to be losing their feet in the crush but as Dick went to make his move, the captain dragged a whistle from his tunic and blew a frantic blast. Gendarmes came running and elbowed their way through the crowd, grabbing the prisoner at the very moment he had managed to free himself.

The tram did not move and the crowd did not go. The people clustered around them, thick, black and menacing. They were menacing his captors and again Dick felt there might be a chance to escape. "*C'est un Anglais!*" shouted the crowd.

The prisoner held his breath thinking that any minute they would rush the gendarmes and the guardes mobiles. The police were too quick, moving in fast with a flourish as they started to swing their batons and beat a way through the crowd. In seconds, Dick was bundled into a taxi and soon the shouting crowd was left far behind, the opportunity lost.

In November 1942 the Germans occupied Vichy France and it was at this time that the Gestapo began to take an unhealthy interest in Dick Cooper at Chambaran. Luckily the camp commandant was given instructions by his French bosses to release Dick and three other agents as quickly as possible.

The four men, all S.O.E. operatives, decided to split up and make their own way to safety. Before parting, they exchanged code numbers to be quoted back home with the information that they were free and on the run. Initially Dick made good time and was helped many times by members of the French farming community in his bid for freedom.

Eventually the pressure of forced marching began to tell on him and particularly on the old injuries to his knees, suffered so many years earlier on the battlefield. Before long the pain was so bad that rest became a major priority.

Heading towards St Victor, Dick came across a tiny church set in the middle of a peaceful cemetery. Although it was late in the season, the sun was still warm and the breezes gentle. In the distance he could see buildings outlining a small village but there were no people. Entering the church with caution, Dick dropped onto a worn wooden pew and inspected the open blisters on his feet. His knees were two large balls of pain and for a while he sat quietly letting the waves of agony wash over his limbs. As the pain began to subside and the harshness of his breathing eased, he looked around the church seeking water with which to bathe and soothe his wounds. For a moment his eyes rested on the leaded font and dragging himself to his feet he took a look into its deep bowl. Yes, there was water in the font and, trusting he was not guilty of sacrilege; he dipped a rag into the water and washed his inflamed skin. In a tiny sacristy he found some towels and these he wrapped around his feet in place of his shredded socks. Praying that God would forgive him, Dick settled down to rest a while in the confessional box. Nevertheless he was frightened to sleep in case someone should come into the church and so he decided to seek a safer hiding place. That night he slept soundly in a cavity behind the altar.

Having laid up for a couple of days, Dick was feeling much better but he was also desperately hungry and so the time had come to make tracks. He needed food and he also needed to get back to Marseilles, where he knew an escape route had been set up. The Germans were now occupying the whole of France so once again he must rely on the help of local people. Taking a chance, he headed for St Victor and a good meal at the local hotel. The people were friendly, and the son of the hotelkeeper was one of many to help him on his way home to England. The young Frenchman went so far as to accompany Dick, by bus, to the town of Tournon where there was a busy railway station.

In Tournon, the station was full of Germans and Italians but Dick had enough confidence in his own spoken French to mingle openly at the booking office. There he discovered that there were no passenger trains available and there were unlikely to be any for about ten days. Dejected, Dick sat on a bench to consider his next move. Trains were constantly passing through the station, crammed either with German soldiers or German machinery. Giving up his immediate plans for going home, the escapee decided it would be an excellent chance to practise his skills in sabotage. The main problem was a lack of the necessary equipment. For some minutes he eyed the locomotives with the professional eye of a wrecker and then, wandering casually through the station, he trudged northwards along the line. He passed by a repair shed with two locomotives inside and further along he came to a signal box on which was written: Tournon, 1k. 500 metres. Through the window he could see the signal man at his post and, just ahead, an engine-less goods train.

The goods wagons, loaded with German equipment, offered the free-lance saboteur just the chance he was seeking. During training they had been warned about being over zealous, that indiscriminate actions could work against the Allied cause but here, in the siding, with the loaded train awaiting the repair of its locomotive was the ideal target. For a while he reconnoitred the area and once he felt reasonably sure that the coast was clear, he filled a couple of discarded sacks with coal dust. Dragging one sack at a time, he made his way along the twenty or so wagons filling the oil boxes on each wheel with the coal dust as he went. Of course he would have preferred sand, apart from anything else it would have been considerably cleaner to work with.

Eventually, well satisfied with his work, Dick made his way to the outskirts of town where he managed to catch a bus just as it was leaving for the town of Valence. They had been rattling along the road for sometime when suddenly the brakes were applied forcefully without warning. Looking from beneath half closed eyelids, the escapee could see a group of gendarmes about to board the bus. The man next to him whispered: "Identity check!" There was no escape. He was trapped.

Two of the gendarmes made their way down the bus checking papers as they went. With a shrug, Dick handed over his military documents and waited for the explosion. Instead, his papers were handed out of the bus to a sergeant who studied them slowly, glancing up occasionally to the window where Dick sat watching.

"Make him come down!" The sergeant barked at his men.

Warily, Dick alighted from the bus that was immediately waved away by the sergeant. As the vehicle rattled on down the road, the gendarmes circled their prey. Not sure what to expect, Dick felt the hairs rise on the back of his neck, his adrenaline surged and his brain leapt to full alert. Forcing himself to stay calm, Dick smiled as the sergeant scrutinised his features. Then the man spoke quietly, friendly, knowingly. "You're Cooper, all right. The description fits, the scar is there." Dick tensed his muscles and, noticing the movement, the man smiled. "Don't worry," he said." You're lucky we found you. A little further down the road you would have been caught at the German checkpoint. You must leave the Drome Department immediately and cross the river to the Ardeche then go south." To Dick's amazement the gendarmes then proceeded to have a whip round and a small bundle of francs was stuffed into his pocket. Quite simply it was one of those inexplicable happenings in wartime that is best accepted without further question.

15 Omega

The Department of the Ardeche was under the control of the
Italian Army and Dick knew that he could easily pass as an
Italian. It was his papers that could put him into danger and
so he needed to be on his guard twenty-four hours a day. He
had to make it to Marseilles and from there to England and
his family. The next stages of his journey took him by various
modes of transport, to Montelimar, Pont St Esprit, southwards
to Avignon, Tarascon to Arles, then branching off to the left
on the road to Aix en Provence and eventually turning due
south to reach his goal, Marseilles.

At last, Dick was in country he knew well and for the first
time in ages he relaxed. It was easy to hop on a bus to the
centre of town where he booked into a small hotel, registering
under the name Jean Debrun (Militaire). Next it was dinner
at a small black market restaurant before taking in a film at
the local picture house. That night Dick Cooper crawled
between cold, snowy white sheets and drifted helplessly into
the deep and dreamless sleep of total exhaustion.

A number of escape routes had been set up from Marseilles
and it was up to Dick to find the most efficient one to get him

home as quickly as possible. After all, he was wasting time wandering about Europe when the war was currently proceeding without him. It was absolutely essential for him to get back to headquarters and seek new instructions.

The next few days were spent in seedy bars and cafes where Dick made discreet enquiries, occasionally dropping in a coded name that had been filed in his memory since his last day of training at Beaulieu. Eventually his persistence paid off when a small, softly spoken, neatly dressed man approached him as he was finishing a cup of coffee in one of the bars.

The newcomer introduced himself as Pat O'Leary and it was some days before Dick realised just how important this inconspicuous man was to the Allied cause. Pat's face betrayed no emotion; his movements were as smooth and agile as a cat. His real name was Albert Guerisse and he was a Belgian doctor who had joined the British Navy. Under the alias of Pat O'Leary he had been sent on a mission to France where he had been quickly captured during the German advance. Before long he had managed to escape by posing as a French workman. Instead of making his way home, Pat had set up one of the most effective escape routes of the war.

Dick was escorted to a house on the heights of Marseilles, just below the Notre Dame de la Garde. Here he was fitted out with a new set of clothes by an ex-inspector of the Paris police. A couple of days later he was issued with a railway ticket for Toulouse. At the Gare St Charles, Dick was joined by a number of other travellers, all taking Pat's underground route to freedom. Overnight, they rested at the Hotel de Paris in Toulouse. The following morning saw the group on another train, this time heading for Perpignan and Cerbere, a tiny village close to the Spanish border.

The final stage of their journey would take them over the Pyrenees and into Spain. Here they were to contact the British consul in Barcelona. However, they were warned, if they fell into Spanish hands then it would result in another spell of internment and Spanish jails were no better than any other. They handed over identity papers and money to be used by those who would surely follow in their footsteps.

It was with some trepidation that the assorted group set out that night to climb the Spanish mountains. They began the march at 8pm when they crossed a dry riverbed to rendezvous with their Spanish guide. The man knew every nook and cranny of the mountains as they climbed higher and higher. None of the escapees were fully fit. Some, like Dick, had spent time in prison camps, living under appalling conditions. The cold bit into their bones and their muscles threatened to seize up. The sounds of their laboured breathing could be heard above the noise of their feet on the stony paths. The night was like pitch and at times the guide warned them of a narrow pass and the sheer drop below. Sometimes a stumbling foot would dislodge a stone and it seemed to take forever before it clattered in the valley. Hours passed, midnight came and went and they had to rest more and more frequently. By two o'clock they were able to make out dim lights gleaming in the distance, the lights of neutral Spain where blackout was unknown.

The sun was rising as they made their way down the last steep incline to a small plateau where they were able to rest their aching limbs throughout the daylight hours. The next night, with supreme effort, they managed to march along a straight road between olive groves, still resting at regular intervals. As daylight filtered through the trees, they sheltered in a disused railway hut. During the long weary hours of the third night, they passed by the town of Figueras heading for the comfort of a farmhouse on the outskirts of a tiny village. Their journey to freedom was very close to its end.

A few days later the press attaché to the Consul-General

arrived at the farm, whisking them all off to Barcelona for Christmas celebrations. Dick was champing at the bit, desperate to get home to England, torn between the desire to see his family and his determination to get back into the theatre of war. At the end of December 1942 the group were taken to the British Embassy in Madrid where Dick managed to borrow £5 to buy some basic clothes to replace his tattered rags. Another few days and they were off again, taken by consular cars to Seville, the next day to Gibraltar and a boat headed for England.

Intelligence officers boarded the boat at Greenock and it was with considerable difficulty that Dick managed to convince them he was a genuine British spy returning home from active duty. For some time the men remained sceptical, apart from their personal desire to trap an enemy agent, the indefinable accent of the new arrival left him wide open to suspicion. Eventually the officers were persuaded to make contact with their own superiors who, after further checks, sent a launch to collect Dick for his debriefing.

Two days and several telegrams later, Dick arrived home in the village of Irchester to the delight of his family. Suddenly he realised how desperately he had missed them all and he was stunned by the change he found in them. Likewise, while Dolly was ecstatic at his return, her happiness was tempered by the appalling condition of his health. During the time they had been apart, Dick had lost more than two stone in weight. Exhaustion was apparent in every movement of his body and the pain of the last eighteen months was clearly evident in the darkness of his eyes and the pallor of his skin.

For several weeks they made the most of their time together, pretending it was one long restful holiday that was never going to end. Dick renewed his acquaintance with his wife who through necessity had matured in his absence to a confident young woman. The children, who had grown in minds as well as bodies, were constantly demanding his attention, oblivious of his exploits and adventures. Gradually he relaxed and as he did so, his health began to improve and with it, his weight and strength. Before too long Dolly had nursed her personal hero back to good health and, inevitably, the summer day arrived when his doctors confirmed that he was fit to return to active duty.

Before he left England a letter arrived addressed to A. R. Cooper and inside he found an invoice. The Embassy in Madrid was reclaiming the £5 lent to him.

This time it was with very mixed feelings that Dick reported for duty. The wrench of parting from his family was far worse than the first time he had left them. On that occasion he had entered with some excitement into the unknown. This time he was fully aware of the dangers he would face and, God help him, of the very precious little world he was leaving behind.

He discovered that his days of operating single-handed behind enemy lines were over. France and Italy were closed to him as an agent as the Gestapo held a dossier on his past activities. However, the Germans were on the run - slowly, bitterly, resisting every step of the way across Sicily and up the leg of Italy but, nevertheless, on the run. The Allies were after them in full cry, slipping their hounds behind their heels to snap, worry, weaken and betray.

Instead of going into action in occupied territories themselves, several members of S.O.E. were detailed to train others for the job. In the chaos that was Sicily and indeed, Italy, it was necessary to recruit suitable men and women of many nationalities and train them as saboteurs, organisers of resistance movements and as political plotters. Finally these brave individuals were tested and only then were they escorted by their teachers to well chosen locations behind enemy lines. Here the recruits would be left to make their own way forward to make their own contacts and then beyond, to the front lines.

In mid-July 1943, Dick was back in action - attached to a group of agents operating from Sicily under the direction of Captain Malcolm Munthe, son of Axel Munthe, author of The Story of San Michelle. Dick was given the name Arturo Ricardo Cavallero, code-name AJ4. These were exhilarating days when they needled the enemy in preparation for the invasion of Italy. Men, operating in peril, determined to destroy the enemy from within. They worked with Italian men and women like Fiametta and Anna, Giovanni and Giuseppe. People with their own individual stories of courage and daring - and often death – all linked by S.O.E. into a cohesive destruction force in the middle of indescribable chaos.

At the beginning of September they heard that Operation Avalanche - the code name for the landings on the Salerno beaches - was imminent. Soon they would be moving their operations to the mainland. Before they left the island Dick put in an urgent request for leave. He was anxious to visit Messina which was still the home of his step sister and step-mother. Perhaps, at last, he would be able to visit his father's grave.

American and British troops were camped along the road from Palermo to Messina and Dick was able to cadge a lift with an American colonel. From the heights above the city they could see across the straits to the mainland, but it was no place to linger in wartime. Great placards had been erected at the roadside and they read: 'If you wish to commit suicide, stay here.' Apparently the Germans shelled across the straits every time they saw a convoy pass. The town was almost deserted when they arrived and Dick could scarcely recognise the place. In peacetime, new houses had been built and now many had been bombed. Messina was reminiscent of 1908 after the earthquake.

Passing more and more demolished buildings, Dick began

to fear for his family and his pace quickened. Reaching the Via San Paolo dei Disciplinanti, he saw windows empty of glass and shutters hanging in splinters. The front door of his sister's home hung limply from twisted hinges. Inside dust and rubble lay everywhere, covering the small treasures that still remained with a fine grey film. On the mantelpiece stood a photograph of his father, the glass broken and the frame splintered. His father's old Indian trunk lay in a corner, the trunk in which Arthur Cooper had always kept his most valued possessions. Dick knelt beside the deeply carved chest and opening the lid he found the family Bible inside, protecting the remaining treasures. His grandmother's wedding dress lay neatly folded, a pair of tiny shoes, papers, documents, photographs. For a while he sat silently in the dust with his past.

A slight breeze disturbed an empty window frame bringing his thoughts back to the present. There was no sign of death in the flat, only marks of a hurried departure. He was sure he would find his step-sister Hetty alive and well somewhere. Pulling the door closed behind him, Dick wedged a piece of broken timber below the handle to keep the door secure. In the Viale San Martino, once the main road, he hailed a passing truck and the driver took him outside the city to a village where he knew his sister had friends. For a while he could find no one who knew of the whereabouts of his family, but his persistence finally paid off. An elderly woman recognised the name of his step mother and suggested he should make enquiries in the village of Giampilieri, a few miles further on.

At Giampilieri he questioned a member of the local carabiniere and was rewarded by a huge smile. His brother-in-law, Giovanni Flaccomio, was an orchestra leader and well-known to the locals. Soon he had an address where he could find his family.

For a moment he stood framed in the doorway of the little village house. Hetty looked up from her sewing to see Bebo grinning down at her. Gazing at him with a mixture of joy and disbelief in her eyes, for a moment his sister could not move and then, with tears trickling down her face, she threw herself into her step-brother's arms.

As they stood in the doorway clinging to each other an inside door opened to reveal his step-mother. Again there were tears and hugs, questions and answers. The next few hours were the most delightful that Bebo had ever spent with any of his family for war had a definite tendency of putting life into perspective. At long last he had some happy memories to be stored.

In the morning, brother and sister set off to visit the cemetery where their father had been laid to rest. The place was indescribable. Bombs must have fallen on it for months and coffins had been blown from the earth. They found their way to the corner where the foreigners were buried. This area had also been devastated. Disinterred bodies lay everywhere and it was almost impossible to walk without tripping over a skeleton. There were five graves in a row and the one on the far right was their father's. At sometime a large bomb must have exploded in front of the section and all five coffins had slid into the crater. They had all burst open and as Hetty and Bebo reached the edge of the hole, they could see their father's remains protruding through a jagged hole in the dark-stained wood.

Hetty fainted and he caught and held her in his arms. For several seconds his own mind and body were numbed. Then, as Hetty recovered consciousness, his resistance broke. They stood together in each others arms weeping.

Slowly they walked to the edge of the cemetery where Dick left his sister to sit on a crumbling wall and wait for him. Taking a deep breath he returned to his father's grave and did what he could to re-inter the remains. Finally he said a short prayer, gave his wry mock salute, and took his sister home for a farewell dinner.

Two days later Dick and a small group of agents were attached to the Fifth Army under the American General Mark Clark, whose command included the British 10th Corps. In a few more days they were deposited on the Salerno beaches in front of Paestum in the 36th U.S. Division sector. Dick had to meet up with Munthe in Salerno and from there, travel on to the island of Capri.

The people on the island showed a great deal of love and respect for the son of their beloved Dr. Axel regarding him as one of their own. Later, Munthe was sent to the liberated town of Naples where he set up his headquarters. Dick, who had been promoted to 'Acting Captain,' now teamed up with another S.O.E. operative known as Dumbo Newton. The two men crossing to the nearby island of Ischia where they set up a very select sabotage school in the castle of Count Fassini at Torre Mezza.

The people they trained were infiltrated through the enemy lines to organise resistance and contact the partisans. Above all they needed to get transmitters to the partisan groups so they could arrange parachute drops of ammunition and explosives. Luckily the German line was so fluid that it was comparatively easy to slip groups through one of the numerous gaps. Many of these sorties proved highly successful but it was a very long time before they were to know this and the actual outcome and value of their efforts.

Accompanying four agents at a time Dick made about fifteen infiltrations during that period. It was the return journey that always proved to be the most dangerous, crossing back through the American line. Although he always ensured that the American officer in charge of the sector was acquainted with his movements, the work was nevertheless top secret and consequently there was always a chance that a trigger-happy G.I. would take a pot shot at him. At the first sign of an American he would yell, "Hold your fire! I'm a British officer." Then there would be a tedious wait at the command post until he was cleared of suspicion.

The work continued successfully but as the weather began to close in so the fluidity of the lines began to disappear. The Germans were settling in for the winter and one of the few places left to infiltrate was a spot between Venafro and Cassino.

Towards the end of 1943 Dick was working with Captain Max Sylvester, an Italian patriot whose real name was Massimo Salvadori. They were attempting to get a large sum of money through the lines to local partisans, sending two recently trained agents as couriers.

The group reached Venafro late one evening, spending the night at the headquarters of a unit of the British 13th Corps. Early the next morning they entered a village of some five hundred inhabitants, which lay on a high promontory at the foot of Monte Arcalone, one of the ranges of mountains which dominate Venafro. The observation post of an American mortar unit occupied the village; behind which lay no man's land and the Germans. The captain in charge of the observation post warned them that an attempt to infiltrate to the left would be hopeless. The enemy was entrenched in great numbers. They decided to slip the men through to the right of the Sammucro River.

Making good use of the daylight hours Dick and Max went to reconnoitre. Climbing down a steep path to the valley below, they crossed a gently meandering stream and headed towards a dilapidated farmhouse standing at the crossroads. With considerable care they entered the building, looking for tell tale signs of booby traps as they went. Once they had satisfied themselves that the place was unlikely to explode,

Max set about sketching the terrain for the benefit of the two young recruits.

The four of them set out late that evening. Moving as silently as possible, they entered no-man's land. The crackling of a dry branch under foot sounded like an explosion in the crisp night air and none of them dared to risk as much as a cough or sneeze.

After a while they took a small path to the right and passed by the gaunt looking farmhouse. Checking their position, they decided the time had come for them to part company. Handing over the maps and giving some last minute instructions, Dick and Max shook hands with the agents and giving a last thumbs up, turned to re-trace their steps.

Carefully in the darkness they made their way back to the observation post. For a while they both leaned over the parapet trying to pinpoint the area they had just left. Listening, hoping the two agents would get through. All was quiet and eventually they turned away, sure that all was well. The huge explosion took them by surprise, so sure they had been that their trainees were safe. Spinning on his heel, Dick was just in time to see an outline of the farm before the flash of light was extinguished.

"A mine has exploded," Max said quietly. "Let's go and see if we can help."

Using all their experience and expertise, Dick and Max made it back to the valley in double quick time. Quietly they criss-crossed the area searching for the two men they had so recently left. Finally they had to give up; they had been in the area for far too long. As they turned, the sound of running feet could be heard and, without a word, they melted into the landscape. A second later, one of the trainees ran straight past them and he was obviously heading for the observation post. For some minutes Dick and Max waited silently and once they were satisfied the man had not been followed, they made a stealthy retreat.

As they had guessed, a mine had exploded killing one of their agents. The other man had been too petrified to move for a while. When he did pluck up some courage, he had run like a bat out of hell, passing them on the way.

As the winter sun raised the first fragile stream of daylight, Max and Dick took a stretcher party down to the farmhouse. They had taken the precaution of inviting a small party of armed American soldiers for protection. Dick was scouting about fifty yards ahead of the others when suddenly he stopped dead in his tracks. Ahead was a group of mutilated cows and beyond was the man they had been seeking. The agent, half sitting, half lying against a tree was obviously dead. The hairs stood up on the back of his neck as Dick realised that he was surrounded by S-mines and anti-personnel mines. In his anxiety to find the missing man he had walked straight into the middle of a mine field.

Throwing caution to the wind, Dick shouted a warning to the others. Turning on the spot and studying the ground carefully, he could see where he had weaved his way safely among the mines. 'How the hell did I manage that?' he thought gratefully.

The grass was wet and thankfully he could still see his own footprints. Placing his feet with meticulous accuracy in each mark, slowly and fearfully he made his way back to the path and safety. Taking a long deep breath and wiping the sweat from his brow, Dick began to shiver uncontrollably. In his mind he could see Lucy and he could hear her voice, never had he felt her so near to him. Tears began to well up and he brushed them away with the sweat. He could hardly explain to the American army that his childhood nursemaid was somewhere close by. The thought brought a smile to his face and his moment of fear and sadness passed unnoticed.

The Allies were advancing through Italy and Dick was transferred to the Balaclava Mission, an independent group of officers and men operating from Corsica under the command of Major Andrew Croft, D.S.O., M.A. with Captain Ken Carson second in charge and Paddy Davies, R.N.R., the intelligence officer. Malcolm Munthe's little force in Naples had been disbanded and the Special Operation Executive group in Italy became known as No1 Special Forces.

Late in 1944, Dick returned to the Italian mainland to train more agents in the mountain villages of Tuscany. Eventually, the super-human effort he had been putting into every activity began to take its toll. Pains in his head and spine, the result of the injuries received during his imprisonment in Algeria and France became almost unbearable. For a while he continued, refusing to admit to the pain, but the time came when he was at the point of collapse and a doctor was called. Apart from the known injuries and the obvious exhaustion, Dick was found to be also nursing a fracture of the left upper jaw.

Almost immediately Dick Cooper was sent home to England for treatment and, inevitably, a discharge. The War Office granted him the honorary rank of Captain and he finally left the service on 28th February 1945, his forty-sixth birthday.

And so it was, the reason that I could be found in the hospital grounds playing with my friends. My father was just eighteen months into the second half of a lifetime, giving plenty of time for him to settle down and to enjoy his future.

As soon as he had recovered from his injuries my father took himself off to London where he was welcomed back with open arms by the Civil Service. Shortly afterwards the driver of the furniture van deposited me and the dog on the pavement while my mother went ahead to inspect our new home.

The years ahead were happy if somewhat uneventful and Dick Cooper travelled the world in his armchair, speaking over the telephone to people in all corners of the globe. He became an inveterate letter writer and corresponded with former members of S.O.E. and with many of the people he had trained in the field. Occasionally there would be a reunion at the Special Forces Club when the stories would expand as the evening progressed.

In the mid nineteen fifties my father was persuaded to write about his many exploits while serving with the Special Operations Executive and the book, entitled The Adventures of a Secret Agent, was eventually published in 1957.

Having completed his service as a supervisor and 'model employee' of the Continental Telephone Exchange, Dick Cooper retired to a small bungalow in a Kentish village where he and Doris could grow roses and delight in the visits of their children and grandchildren. They enjoyed many a long walk with their faithful companion Rusty, a loyal corgi who lived to a very great age. A miniature Aquila, in the form of Verdi – the budgerigar, also enjoyed the comforts of my parent's home.

Our children adored their grandfather and it was surprising just how much time he gave to them. They all know the words of Lucy's Greek lullaby that Granddad sang to them as babies.

Like his father and grandfather my brother excels in languages and, much to our father's delight, Richard also inherited a singing voice from the Italian connection in the family with the result that throughout the years he has given us all a great deal of pleasure with his renditions of Italian arias. Always a chip off the old block, my brother also served with the British Army both in the Royal Artillery and as a reservist in the S.A.S. but that is *his* story to tell.

Meanwhile, it seems that I inherited my father's mischievous mind and wicked sense of humour which I adeptly managed to pass on to my three children, Lori, Scott and Todd; as all who know us will confirm.

By the late nineteen-sixties Dick Cooper was writing again and "Born to Fight" was published in 1969, a book described as the autobiography of a frontline soldier. On the final page of this book he wrote -:

I live a life of leisure at Ditton, on the outskirts of Maidstone in Kent across the Medway from the Carmelite priory at Aylesford. There, on morning walks beside the river and in the evenings, I hear the Brothers at their devotions, reminding me of the White Fathers of Ain Sefra. My Foreign Legion friends of Kenadza and Dar Lahoussine would laugh uproariously if they could surprise me one Sunday in a Kentish lane as I walk with my grandchildren.

I do not think it sad that I survived into old age. Gone are the days when I believed death on the battlefield was a splendid short cut to heaven. For I know the joy of a child's laugh, the thrill of a blackbird's song and the indescribable pleasure of that first whiff of perfume from a rose planted with one's own hands.

Having gained the writing bug and with Doris regaining her typing speeds, "March or Bust," Stories of the Foreign Legion, was published in 1972. Meanwhile many of my father's colleagues were also writing their memoirs with the result that he is mentioned in numerous books about the two World Wars.

Dick Cooper was in his late seventies when two young thugs decided they would take him on, blissfully unaware of the risk that they were personally taking. Crossing a little-used footbridge above the Maidstone railway line instinct told him that he was being followed. Mentally preparing himself for the inevitable onslaught he gripped his snakehead walking stick firmly in his right hand and shoved the small package he was carrying deep into his coat pocket.

Reaching the end of the bridge Dick kept to the footpath and headed quickly towards the town. His would be assailants

239

took their chance as the path crossed a small grassed area but as he turned, stick raised in one hand and his other hand clenched around a few keys, they ran for their lives leaving him chuckling as he rested on a nearby bench.

Towards the end of 1986 my father received a plea for help from a group of Canadian ex-servicemen led by former Sergeant Pilot James Templeton. Apparently the Canadian government had decided to pay pensions to former PoW's with the exception of those imprisoned at the Laghouat camp. The reason for the decision being their belief that, at the time, Algeria was under the control of the Vichy French. For nearly ten years the men had unsuccessfully tried to prove the case until Templeton, whose aircraft had crashed while he was serving with RAF Bomber Command, remembered their fellow inmate Dick Cooper.

During the lengthy correspondence that preceded a successful outcome, my father was somewhat bemused to discover that this same group of Canadians had planned to kill him while imprisoned at Laghouat. Apparently there had been a collaborator at the camp who had been passing information to the guards. Unable to establish the identity of this traitor they had decided it must be my father. Their logic being based on the slight accent with which this Englishman spoke his own language and also on the number of languages he was able to speak fluently.

From many hundreds of miles away in England my mother, unknowingly, had taken actions that were to save the life of her husband. Having wiled away the long lonely evenings knitting socks she had made up a parcel of these with other goodies, photographs and letters to send to my father by way of the Red Cross. It was the timely arrival of this parcel that had convinced his colonial cell mates that he was a genuine prisoner, but only after they had drawn straws and decided exactly which one of them would kill him. My father found the whole story thoroughly amusing and with a twinkle in his eye I watched him take a quick look towards heaven and, no doubt, his guardian angel.

It was on Good Friday 1988 that Dick Cooper left us to go and look for Lucy. I have not the slightest doubt that he found her for I know that she was never very far away!

Captain Cooper and family

The Cooper children - from left Wilfred, Adolphus, Daisy

Lucy

Arthur Cooper

Dick Cooper on board the Fiora

Aisha the mule

Dick Cooper aged 17 wearing Croix de Guerre

Aquila the eagle

Katoushka and pups

Osman Iki and pup Azer

Dick Cooper aged 84